THE MILITANTS

A Play

by

NORMAN HOLLAND

SAMUEL  FRENCH

LONDON

NEW YORK   TORONTO   SYDNEY   HOLLYWOOD

ISBN 0 573 01274 1

MADE AND PRINTED IN GREAT BRITAIN BY
WHITSTABLE LITHO LTD., WHITSTABLE, KENT

For Thora, Roger and Trevor -
all natives of Metringham.

CHARACTERS

Representing the Oppressors

Alderman Joseph Malin, Mayor-elect of Metringham
Reuben Randall, Liberal agent for Metringham
P.C. Thomas Dougan
Inspector Nathan Arkwright

Representing the Sympathizers with the Oppressed

Richard Ward, Liberal candidate for Metringham

Representing the Oppressed

Nelly Brown, maid-of-all-work to the Malins
Minnie Brown, her sister
Rachel Randall, wife to Reuben Randall
Lilian Malin, wife to Josiah Malin
Vivian Malin, daughter to Josiah Malin
Sophie Ormesby, cousin to Lilian
Lady Honoria Cumberleigh
Eulalia Powle
"Captain" Ada Leyland
Sundry Suffragettes

The action of the play takes place in the drawing-room of Alderman Malin's home and in the street immediately outside it

ACT I
  The evening of 23rd April 1908

ACT II
  Scene 1   Evening of 24th April 1908
  Scene 2   A few minutes later

ACT III
  Late afternoon and evening of 25th April 1908

AUTHOR'S NOTE

Conceivably, some groups might be tempted to go all out to play the suffragettes for broad comedy from the outset. This would be wrong because the prevailing mood is one of sincerity.

The goal of female franchise would have been a difficult one for the suffragettes to attain in the face of the adamant Establishment if they had been supported by a fully-equipped Army and Navy. But they had only themselves: inventive, determined and dedicated. They often seemed both pitiful and comic in the struggle against Law and Order. Sometimes, however, they succeeded in turning the tables so that politicians and police appeared foolish and confounded. The happenings in Metringham during those three April days of 1908 chronicle just one of those occasions.

"The Militants" *are* absurd and amusing when measured against the background of our times; they even seemed absurd when measured against the background of their own times, their limitations and the enormity of their mission. In a word, like all truly comic characters, they were incongruous.

A small point: it may be that, in a particular group, one of the other players is better equipped to sing the song which opens the meeting. In that case, Honoria has only to switch the name when she introduces the song.

Local conditions may render it difficult for the whole of the song to be delivered at the end of the play in which case it is best to cut at the repetition of "This is the Land" and then go straight into "We Shall Overcome."

N. H.

Words of the song "Is this the Land?" by Norman Holland. Music by Trevor T. Smith.

Music for the two songs is available from Samuel French Ltd

ACT I

The composite setting enables one to see not only the hall and drawing-room of the home of Alderman Josiah Malin, Mayor-elect of Metring-ham, but also the street immediately outside his house. The street comprises the fore-stage and a section of the street which runs up the right-hand side of the house so that the area is, in effect, L-shaped. There is an entrance down R leading into the street and another down L where the entrance appears to be from a covered entry over the arch of which is a hanging lamp—now lit. The wall supporting the arch marks the extremity of the setting and a window is set half-way down the wall. At the top of the L is an imposing front door with a brass knocker and this is flanked by shrubs in tubs. Within the house, the door admits to a hall. The rest of the setting is the drawing-room. A short flight of stairs leads down from a landing with an unseen corridor leading off it. A door leads from the room to the other ground-floor rooms. Throughout, the front door is so described and this other door receives no qualification. The street and the house are not divided physically but the interior of the house, when lit, is always illumined by a golden glow whilst the street lighting is a greeny-yellow typical of provincial gas-lit streets around the turn of the century. The action of the play strays from in the house to outside in the street and the shift of interest is always indicated—sometimes one area is blacked out and occasionally the action is frozen in one area so as to concentrate attention on the more important of two phases of happening.

When the CURTAIN rises, the street is lit, with the house in darkness. Two young women enter R. Stealthily, they creep down the street until they reach a spot with a clear view of the front door. Furtively they glance behind them and then peer in the direction of the arch. Reassured, they relax. Nelly and Minnie Brown are sisters, small and determined girls. Nelly, at twenty-two, is the elder and the more spectacularly dressed of the two: a large feathered hat, a feather boa and a dashing two-piece costume complete the outfit. Minnie, two or three years younger, is sombrely dressed in clothes considered appropriate to a working class girl in 1908. •

Nelly Right then, our Minnie. When I say three.

Both girls visibly brace themselves

   One—two—three!

Nellie
Minnie   *Down with Win-ston Chur-chill!* $\left\{\begin{array}{l}\textit{shouting}\\\textit{together}\end{array}\right.$

Tensely, they await a reaction. There is none. They relax

Minnie Do you think he heard us?

Nelly Don't be stupid—Winston Churchill is in Manchester.

Minnie I didn't mean him. I meant him in there. (*Pointing to the house*) I meant Alderman Malin.

Nelly Perhaps he's out. Perhaps he's at the club. We'll try again. Both bits this time. One—two—three . . .

Nelly
Minnie   *Votes for Women! Down with Win-ston Chur-chill!* {*shouting together*

They turn and look fearfully towards the front door. It remains closed. They register disappointment. Then Nelly glances in the direction of the arch and reacts

Nelly There he is! There's Mr Malin—and he's coming this way!

Nelly grabs her sister by the arm and hustles her off by the way they entered

Voices are heard indicating the approach of some persons to the arch on the L

Josiah (*off*) Now, Reuben. Now. Keep it down, lad. Keep it down.

Reuben (*off*) I'm going to sing. I'm going to sing if hell has me.

Reuben comes spinning drunkenly through the arch and sways to a wavering halt when he gives out with a great bellow which is a prelude to his burst of song. Josiah follows closely

> Oooo—oh! (*He starts to dance clumsily as he sings*)
> She's a bright lass and a bonny lass
> And she loves her beer
> And they call her Cushy Butterfield
> And I wish she was here.

Josiah dashes up and seizes Reuben as he is embarking on a more ambitious—and more unsteady—dance routine

Josiah Stop it! This is where I live! I won't have it! I won't have it it here! (*He, too, is drunk but the drink seems merely to have heightened his habitual pomposity*)

Reuben That's a Geordie song. My mother was a Geordie.

Josiah I don't care if she was King Edward's auntie. I'm not having that bloody row on my doorstep. Kindly remember that I'm Mayor-elect of this town. Will you promise to keep quiet?

Reuben (*nodding*) Promise.

Josiah releases Reuben. Now, as Josiah stands regarding Reuben doubtfully, we are able to appreciate the gulf which divides the two men: Alderman Josiah Malin, consciously successful, dark-suited, bowler-hatted, gold watch chained, and bearing about him that aura of conscious superiority and merited privilege peculiar to some aldermen at the beginning of the twentieth century: Reuben Randall, rebellious, fortyish and shabby-genteel (more shabby than genteel) has yet to discover whether he drinks because he is a failure or whether he is a failure because he drinks. Reuben looks back in the direction of the arch

Where is he? Where's the candidate?

Josiah (*peering in the same direction and taking a step or two towards the arch*) He was close behind us. Here he is. Come along, Mr Ward.

Richard Ward strolls towards them. He is young, elegant and smartly dressed—wears gloves and carries a cane. The other two are dowdy provincials by comparison. Richard is clearly the sophisticated product of the metropolis

Reuben Thought we'd lost you, Mr Ward.

Richard I saw no occasion to hurry—and I could certainly hear you.

Reuben (*mimicking*) "I could certainly hear you." (*Then, anxious not to give offence*) Oh, take no notice of me. I like you, Mr Ward. I do—I like you. But shall I tell you—shall I tell you what I said to myself when I first saw you?

Josiah Now, Reuben. Now . . .

Reuben I said to myself: "Sir Walter's sent us a right toffy-nosed Southerner as prospective Liberal candidate for Metringham." That's what I said. (*He belches*) That's what I said to myself.

Josiah Here, hold on, Reuben.

Richard Thank you very much. Would you be interested in my first impression of you, Mr Randall?

Reuben No, no, listen. I've changed my mind. I've changed my mind about you. Sir Walter knew what he was doing when he chose you as his successor. If anybody can keep Metringham a Liberal seat, it's you. (*He belches again*)

Josiah (*seizing Richard by his coat lapel*) Mind you, you'll need guidance——

Reuben seizes him by the other lapel and the two men pull Richard this way and that as they seek to impress him with the force and cogency of their arguments

Reuben —from those more experienced than yourself.

Josiah You'll need advice——

Reuben —from those who recognize the pitfalls.

Josiah The pitfalls and the dangers.

Reuben You'll need to listen——

Josiah —to those who know what's what.

Reuben If you accept guidance——

Josiah —and listen to advice——

Reuben —there's no reason why, in time——

Josiah —you shouldn't be as good a Member——
Reuben —as solid and sound a Member——
Josiah —as Sir Walter himself.

Richard frees himself and smooths down his lapels

Richard Thank you, gentlemen, I'll bear in mind what you have said.
Reuben Any man who can outdrink Josiah Malin *and* me is qualified to represent this ancient borough in the Mother of Parliaments.
Richard It's very kind of you to say so.
Reuben It's no more than the truth. I'll tell you something: you've more chance of being elected Member for Metringham than Winston Churchill has of being returned for North Manchester.
Josiah Come off it, Reuben! Winston Churchill's the ablest politician on either side of the House.
Reuben I'm in full agreement: Minister at thirty-one, Privy Councillor at thirty-two, and now President of the Board of Trade. But the suffragettes will have him out.
Josiah Have him out? A pack of screaming women? Do you really know who you're talking about? Winston Churchill, that's who. He was in the charge at Omdurman. He fought the Boers—men eight feet tall—with bloody beards as long as you. You don't think he'll concern himself with shrieking bitches, do you?
Reuben No, I don't.
Josiah There you are then.
Reuben That's where he'll be wrong.
Josiah Now look at it sensibly—if you can. Two years ago he won North Manchester by twelve hundred and forty-one votes. Now, having been appointed a Minister of the Crown, he comes back, according to custom, to seek confirmation of his candidature from his—his constituents.
Reuben And a very stupid arrangement if you ask me.
Josiah It's no more than a vote of confidence. He's up against Joynson Hicks, the same opponent as last time, and you're not going to persuade me that Joynson Hicks has become that much more popular with the electors of North Manchester. No, it's Winston for me—with an increased majority.
Reuben They left him alone last time. Now Sylvia Pankhurst is up here. Christabel Pankhurst is up here. Next thing we know Mrs Emmeline Pankhurst will be here. You ought to hear 'em at his meetings. Interruptions inside and outside the hall. I'll tell you what I'll do. You're a rich man and I'm a poor one.
Josiah Not rich, Reuben. I'm not rich—just well-to-do.
Reuben I'll bet you five golden sovereigns that Winston Churchill loses this election.
Josiah Shame on you—to bet against your own party! And you the Liberal agent for Metringham. It's downright disloyalty. Before your own prospective candidate, too.

Reuben Is it a bet?

Josiah Well, if you've the money to throw away . . .

Reuben I've not. But I'm sure I'll win.

Josiah Then I'll shame you. I'll give you ten to one—fifty sovereigns against five to show you what *I* think of Winston's chances.

Reuben takes out a small notebook and pencil, makes a note and restores both articles to his pocket

Have you made a note of that bet?

Reuben I have that.

Josiah I'm surprised your hand didn't drop off while you were writing it.

They are startled by a sudden uproar and clangour: the loud clatter of hooves and the louder ringing of a fire-bell as a fire-engine sweeps by close at hand

Reuben There's a fire somewhere or other.

Josiah You must be a fortune-teller. Well, it's no good standing here. Are you coming in?

Reuben Not me, thanks, Josiah. A political agent's work is never done. I ought to show my face at the Liberal Club for an hour or two.

Josiah That should clear the place in ten seconds flat.

Reuben Then I'll say good-bye for now,, Mr Ward. (*He offers Richard his hand*) I think you'll do well here.

Richard Thank you. You're very kind.

Reuben Good night, Josiah. (*He moves away in the direction of the archway*)

Josiah Reuben . . .

Reuben (*pausing*) Yes?

Josiah If you go to the Liberal Club in that state, you'll have a terrible head in the morning.

Reuben I've always got a terrible head in the morning.

Reuben exits through the archway

Josiah Poor Reuben! He's his own worst enemy. Let's go in.

Richard and Josiah go towards the house, the distant shrilling of a police whistle is heard. Richard pauses and checks Josiah

Richard What's that?

Josiah (*listening*) I can't hear anything.

Richard I thought I heard a police whistle.

Josiah Not round here. This is a respectable neighbourhood.

Richard and Josiah move towards the front door

Rachel Randall enters the street from R. She is an ageing, harassed, shabby woman, still trying to maintain a respectable appearance though she realizes that the odds are heavily against her

Rachel Mr Malin . . .

Anticipating a private discussion, Richard makes a small, tactful withdrawal as Rachel and Josiah advance towards each other

Josiah Yes, Mrs Randall.

Rachel Have you seen Reuben? They said he was with you.

Josiah He was here not a minute ago.

Rachel Where was he going? Did he say?

Josiah Yes, he said he was going to the Liberal Club.

Rachel I've been there twice already. I should have waited—he's always there sometime during the evening.

Josiah Is anything the matter, Mrs Randall?

Rachel Only the usual—the usual with me, that is. I've got the bailiffs in—for debt. It's the grocer who put them in—the one who delivers whisky and bottled beer for Reuben. It seems he hasn't been paid.

Josiah How much is it?

Rachel Now, Mr Malin, you've been very good but I can't . . .

Josiah I tell you this—he hasn't got any money.

Rachel I never expected he would have but I'd like him to know about the bailiffs. Is that being bitter and revengeful?

Josiah If it is, you've got good reason . . .

Rachel Because I feel bitter and revengeful. Yes, and humiliated.

Josiah You haven't told me how much it is. Come now, I know the money will be safe with you. (*He takes some money from his pocket*)

Rachel It's five pounds, thirteen shillings and threepence. You can get a lot of beer and whisky for that. But then, Reuben's a thirsty man.

Josiah (*putting the money in her hands*) There's six pounds. I'll get it back from Reuben.

Rachel Oh, I'll take it. I've no choice. But when you'll get it back, I can't promise. It's worse than I've told you. We were saving up to go to Scarborough at Wakes Week. He's spent the lot. I only found out this afternoon.

Josiah It'll sort itself out. You'll see. And don't worry. You must meet Mr Ward who is the prospective Liberal candidate.

Richard comes down to them

Richard (*offering his hand*) How do you do, Mrs Randall.

Rachel (*taking Richard's hand*) I'm sorry, Mr Ward. So sorry that you should have to hear all that. I've never felt so ashamed in my life.

Richard Why should you? These things happen in the best regulated households.

Rachel Ours is not one of the best regulated households and this happens all too often as Mr Malin will confirm. Thank you, Mr Malin, for helping us yet again. I'll go and get rid of the bailiffs. (*She starts to leave but turns to look back at Richard*) Reuben wasn't always like this, Mr Ward. I believe his drinking started after our little girl died. But there's a good man still somewhere inside Reuben Randall and he's very good company—when he's out.

Rachel exits

Josiah (*gazing sadly after her*) She's wrong, you know. Reuben Randall was a drinker from the very beginning. She thought she could reform him.

Richard and Josiah go to the front door. Josiah opens the door with his key, and they pass through into the drawing-room. As they go, the drawing-room lights up, and the lighting in the street goes out

Richard (*looking round*) Very pleasant place you've got here.
Josiah It's homely. It's comfortable and it's solidly built. You've no houses like this in London. What will you have to drink? Whisky? Rum? Gin?
Richard A drop of whisky wouldn't come amiss.
Josiah I'll say this for you, young man—you can certainly shift the whisky. Here, sit down. Make yourself comfortable.

Richard sits in one of the armchairs

Water or soda?
Richard Soda, please.
Josiah (*pouring*) One of the womenfolk'll be here in a minute. Here you are. (*He passes the drink to Richard*) That all right?
Richard Thank you, yes.

Josiah returns to the sideboard to mix his own drink

Josiah It's the wife's night for Bible studies. She has to set an example.
Richard I see what you mean—with you being Mayor-elect.
Josiah I'm a great believer in Bible sayings. "Let your light so shine before men. . . ." Did you notice the horse-trough as we came past the Hippodrome?
Richard How could I help it? You drew my attention to it *and* to the fact that your name was carved on it as the donor.
Josiah (*sitting in the other armchair*) That's right. Every so often I manage to pass that way as the audience is leaving the Hippodrome. I let them see me. By the horse-trough. Just to remind them that I'm a public benefactor.
Richard The water in the trough looked pretty slimy to me.

Josiah Never mind that. I'll tell you something else. You must have been impressed by the new Town Hall we're building.

Richard I was. I have never seen such an architectural monstrosity.

Josiah Be that as it may. It suits us. The new Town Hall will be opened during my year of office. Royalty will preside over the opening ceremony and *my* name will be carved on the stone over the entrance. I'll be confirmed as the leading public figure in Metringham.

Richard Is that what you want then?

Josiah Wouldn't anybody want that? I'm a successful tradesman—sixteen grocers' shops in this part of Lancashire and it'll be twenty before I die. But is that enough? There's something else in life besides material things.

Richard Ah, yes! "Man's reach must exceed his grasp or what's a heaven for?"

Josiah (*impressed*) That's very clever. I wouldn't have thought you had it in you.

Richard Oh, it's not mine. Browning said that.

Josiah A friend of yours?

Richard I like to think so.

They drink ruminatively

Are you a family man, Mr Malin?

Josiah Yes, I've the best wife and daughter in the world.

Richard I hope you tell them so.

Josiah Tell them so? Listen, I'll give you some good advice: never let them know that you're fond of them or they'll take advantage and you'll end up not able to call your soul your own.

Richard I don't agree. If you love somebody, you tell them—and go on telling them.

Josiah You say that because you're young, rash, inexperienced and *wrong!*

Richard shakes his head in contradiction but, catching Josiah's eye and realizing the futility of further argument, changes the subject

Richard Do you think Reuben's right?

Josiah Right?

Richard About the suffragettes. Are they really damaging Churchill's chances? After all, it was here, in neighbouring Manchester that they started.

Josiah It was and it's a lasting disgrace. They ought to have stamped them out at the very outset. Do you know what I'd do if I had my way?

Richard What?

Josiah I'd have Sylvia and Christabel Pankhurst put in prison until they mended their ways. Then I'd have them both flogged and put on bread and water. As for Mrs Emmeline Pankhurst, I'd put her in solitary confinement—in the dark, mind—and she'd have neither crust nor drink until she promised to disband the suffragettes. And then do you know what I'd do?

Richard No. What?

Josiah I'd have her sentenced to ten years hard labour without remission. That's what I'd do.

Richard I see. (*He sips his whisky*) Have you always been a Liberal, Mr Malin?

Josiah Always. All my life—and my father before me. For him, Billy Gladstone was the greatest man who ever lived. He was, too, wasn't he?

Richard Oh, I don't know. There are others worthy of consideration: Jesus Christ, Michelangelo, Beethoven, Mohammed, Shakespeare . . .

Josiah I'm not talking about foreigners. I don't reckon them.

Richard But Shakespeare . . .

Josiah Yes, yes. I know. Shakespeare was English but he was always writing about foreigners.

Richard Not all the time.

Josiah Often enough.

Richard Mr Malin, I wonder if you realize the danger here. I'm told that Metringham is a hotbed of suffragettes.

Josiah It may be. But it won't be for long. I'll have 'em put down. You'll see.

Richard I understand they're very well organized here. Haven't they a leader called Hippolyta?

Josiah Called what? I've never heard of her. Hippolyta! What's that mean?

Richard Hippolyta was the ancient Queen of the Amazons. In olden times she fought against the race of men.

Josiah Did she? Did she now? Well, today she is likely to get her bottom smacked. Mr Ward, I'm a progressive man. (*Indicating*) That's why I installed the telephone. (*He rises and draws himself up to his full height*) I'm a fair man, a tolerant man, a far-seeing man, a man of wide and varied experience and I tell you, in all sincerity, that women just aren't fitted to have the vote. They're made different from us.

Richard They are indeed.

Josiah They're simply not logical thinking creatures. Women have their place—two places, in fact. (*He draws a deep breath as a preliminary to a profound announcement*)

Richard
Josiah In the kitchen and in bed. $\begin{cases} speaking \\ together \end{cases}$

Josiah I see. You've heard it before.

Richard Wasn't it something Gladstone said in eighteen-eighty-nine?

Josiah I don't think so. He was a bit of a Holy Joe. But I had a speech—a wonderful speech—on the unsuitability of women as electors.

Richard When did you deliver it?

Josiah That's just it. I didn't. I was to have delivered it at the Mechanics' Hall in February but . . .

Richard But?

Josiah Just as I got into my stride, the hall filled with smoke.

Richard No!

Josiah True as I stand here. It was the suffragettes. They filled the cellar with smouldering rags and the audience ran out choking and screaming, "Fire!" I had a sore throat for weeks.

Richard How did you know it was them?

Josiah They shouted, "Votes for Women," when the confusion was at its height and left the hall with the rest of the public. They didn't catch a single one of them.

Richard It's just as I said. They're highly organized.

Josiah Maybe they are. But they've me to reckon with and I'll put 'em down. I'll not have it—not in my own town. I've still got the speech in my study—I'll go and get it for you.

Richard Oh, please don't put yourself to the trouble.

Josiah No trouble at all. You might be able to use some of it when you start your campaign. I won't be above a few minutes.

Josiah exits by the door

Richard shrugs resignedly and rises, glass in hand, He goes over to the plant, empties his glass into the plant-pot, and stands listening as a police whistle shrills again, nearer this time. As if the whistle was a signal, the street lights up, but less brightly than before.

In the street. P.C. Thomas Dougan strolls into view R. *He is a man of immense dignity—a dignity enhanced by a magnificent set of whiskers. He stands, a monument of the law, surveying the scene. He watches all that follows with something between concern and Olympian detachment: shaking his head sorrowfully, raising his eyes Heavenward, massively shrugging his shoulders, casting wide his arms as if deploring female wrongdoing while refusing to accept any responsibility for it. He makes no attempt to detain them or disclose himself*

Headlong through the arch comes Nelly Brown. Her large feather hat has fallen forward over her face. She halts, out of breath, adjusts her hat and, relieved that she is not followed, thumbs her nose at the invisible pursuit. A police whistle sounds again and, startled, she plunges forward, rummaging in her bag. As she reaches the front door she finds the key, opens the door and hurries into the house, her hat again flopping over her face. She raises it, and finds herself within inches of Richard

Nelly Oo-er! Remember you haven't seen nobody!

*Nelly runs swiftly past Richard, up the stairs and out of sight.
Richard gazes at her.*
*In the Street. Now it seems that two police whistles are sounding
together as Miss Sophie Ormesby scuttles into view through the
arch. She is not exactly running, but she is walking very fast and
still contriving to preserve her middle-aged dignity. As far as we
can make out, she appears to be somewhere in the neighbourhood
of fifty. She, too, makes a bee-line for the front door, opens it, and
hurries into the house*

Richard turns with a start, to find Sophie confronting him

Sophie Ssh! Not a word! Not a word!

Sophie vanishes up the stairs.

*In the street. Now, to a positive concert of police whistles, Vivien
Malin scurries through the arch. She turns, glances behind her, and
dashes to the front door*

*Richard pours himself a whisky. Vivien opens the front door with her
key, slams the door, and, arms outstretched, leans against it as if to
keep out her pursuers. Almost at the limit of her endurance, she closes
her eyes and strives to recover her breath. After a moment or two she
opens her eyes and sees Richard, glass in hand, observing her with un-
blinking interest. She is well worth his attention—a vivid and striking
girl*

Vivien Oh! Oh! What are you doing here?
Richard I'm Richard Ward. You remember—we met yesterday.
Vivien Yes, yes. By the Corn Exchange.
Richard Your father brought me here. I didn't realize you were . . .
Vivien Where is he?
Richard Through there—in his study.

*Vivien, with her eyes fixed on the door by which her father must return,
dashes to the foot of the stairs, and turns to Richard*

Vivien I wasn't here. You haven't seen me.

Vivien flashes up the stairs and disappears

Richard takes a pull at his drink

Josiah enters with a sheaf of papers in his hands

Richard chokes

Josiah Did I hear voices?
Richard I was just humming to myself.
Josiah I'm surprised you're not singing at the top of your voice

after all you've drunk tonight. Here, sit down. (*He thrusts the speech into Richard's hand*)

Richard sits

Read there. (*He points*) Read this passage. That'll give you some idea.

Richard settles to read. Josiah strolls round the room striving to appear jauntily unconcerned, but really looking self-consciously proud and pleased with himself

In the street. Police whistles shrill near at hand, and Inspector Nathan Arkwright dashes full-tilt through the arch. He is carrying an inspector's stick and has a bloodstained handkerchief wrapped round the thumb of one hand. When he sees P.C. Dougan he checks abruptly

Nathan A gang of women. Which way? Which way did they go? (*He moves as if to plunge off* R)

Dougan magisterially raises a hand to halt the Inspector, then with the same hand points precisely to the door of the house, and then, still using the same hand, holds up one finger, two fingers, three fingers

In there? Impossible, man!

Dougan nods in confirmation. Doubtfully, Nathan approaches the front door and turns again to look at Dougan, who nods once more with increasing gravity. Reassured, Nathan raises the knocker and raps out a sharp rat-tat-tat

Josiah pauses and looks at the front door. Richard glances up from his reading. Nelly enters from the door—neat in black dress, white cap and apron, the very model of a demure maid-servant

Nelly (*curtsying*) Shall I see who it is, sir?
Josiah Yes, Nelly. But don't let 'em in.

Nelly goes to the front door

They come bothering me at all hours.
Richard Yes, I suppose they do.

Nelly opens the front door and holds a whispered conversation with Nathan. She appears taken aback by what he says, signifies that he is to wait while she reports to her master, and returns to Josiah

Josiah (*irritably*) Who is it?
Nelly It's Inspector Arkwright, sir. He says three women—suffragettes—were seen coming into the house just now.
Josiah What's this? Ask him to come in.

*But Nathan has heard and comes in leaving the front door open behind
him. Richard rises*

Nathan (*saluting as he comes forward*) Sorry to disturb you, sir. But
I am given to understand that three women who took part in the
suffragette disturbance this evening have taken refuge in your
house. They were seen to enter by the front door.

Josiah When was this, Nathan?

Nathan Not three minutes ago, sir. I was right behind them. One
of my men, P.C. Thomas Dougan, reports that he saw them rush
into this house.

Josiah But this is plain ridiculous! We've been in here for the past
ten minutes. I was out of the room for just a moment or two but
Mr Ward has been here the whole time. You do know Mr Ward?

*In the street. P.C. Dougan moves so that he can stand contemplating
the house*

Nathan Yes—met him at the Liberal Club.

Richard Of course.

Josiah Have you seen anybody?

Richard Nobody at all.

Nelly registers relief

Josiah My wife is out at her Bible class. I don't know whether my
daughter and our cousin . . .

*Suddenly, above stairs, there is a burst of music from one of the upper
rooms. A piano plays the opening bars of the accompaniment to "The
Last Rose of Summer" and then a glorious soprano voice is heard
singing*

Vivien (*off*)   'Tis the last rose of summer
                              Left blooming alone;
                              All her lovely companions
                              Are faded and gone.

Josiah Oh, they're in then. (*To Nelly*) Ask them to come down.

Nelly bobs and climbs the stairs. The song continues

I don't understand. (*He notices the bloodied handkerchief wrapped
around Nathan's thumb*) Here, what's the matter with your hand?

Nathan I've been bitten.

Josiah Bitten?

Nathan I caught one of them in that dark alley behind the Fish
Market. The bitch grabbed my hand and bit my thumb—practi-
cally to the bone. I let her go, of course, and she was the one I
was following when . . .

Josiah I can't believe it. I just can't believe that so-called civilized
women can behave like this. It's not natural.

Nathan You don't know them. Something's happened to women. They're going berserk. They have no respect for the law. This (*He holds up his swathed hand*) is only a beginning. It will end with them having to call on the military.

The song ceases abruptly

Josiah I hope not—that would be admitting that the situation is getting out of hand.
Nathan It's pretty near that already. We haven't enough police to cope with them. They set fire to the contents of upwards of thirty pillar-boxes tonight.
Josiah Good God in Heaven!
Nathan *And* they set fire to the Mechanics' Hall.
Josiah They didn't!
Nathan Somebody did—and I don't think it was the Church Lads Brigade. Terrorism—that's their weapon. They've got a leader and she knows what she's doing.
Josiah Yes. Hippolyta.
Nathan Hip-what?
Josiah That's what they call their leader—Hippolyta. She was Queen of the Amazons.
Nathan Was she now?

Vivien and Sophie appear side by side on the stairs—their hands folded before them—each the personification of submissive womanhood

Sophie You wanted us, Cousin Josiah.
Josiah Yes, Sophie. It's something and nothing. You know the Inspector. This is Mr Ward, prospective Liberal candidate for the borough. My wife's cousin, Miss Ormesby. My daughter Vivien.

Richard bows. The ladies give a gracious inclination of the head in unison

There's been trouble. The suffragettes have set fire to—how many was it?
Nathan Over thirty.
Josiah Over thirty pillar-boxes.
Sophie Oh! $\left\{\begin{array}{l}speaking\\together\end{array}\right.$
Vivien

They turn and face each other with an expression of alarm

Josiah *And* they've fired the Mechanics' Hall.
Sophie Ah! $\left\{\begin{array}{l}speaking\\together\end{array}\right.$
Vivien

And each one raises her hand to her face in a similar shocked gesture

Josiah Inspector Arkwright was chasing some of them. He caught one but she got away.

Sophie How dreadful!

Josiah And he thinks she came in here with two other suffragettes.

Vivien Oh, no, Father! (*She goes down the stairs and, apparently frightened, hurries over to her father*) Are they in the house? Will they burn it down?

Josiah (*comforting her*) No, no. There's no danger. Have you seen anybody?

Vivien No, Father.

Josiah (*to Sophie*) Did you hear anything?

Sophie Not lately. We heard the fire-engine earlier on. We had just started Vivien's music lesson.

Josiah Yes, yes. We heard. (*He releases Vivien*) I think I'd like a word with that P.C. Thomas Dougan of yours, Nathan.

Josiah goes out through the front door. Nathan follows

In the street. Dougan salutes as he moves to greet the Mayor-elect and his Inspector. The three men congregate some little distance from the arch. We cannot hear what is being said but Josiah is clearly indignant. Nathan appears to be occasionally interjecting a reprimand, while P.C. Dougan seeks to defend himself by reaffirming his earlier statement. This seems to incense the others who grow visibly more heated. P.C. Dougan remains calm, impassive and spectacularly irritating

Sophie We are very grateful, Mr Ward. However, it is only what I would have expected of you.

Richard But you don't know me, Miss Ormesby.

Sophie Ah, there's knowing, Mr Ward, and there's recognition.

This cryptic utterance obviously puzzles the young people

Are you coming, Vivien?

Vivien. In a moment, Cousin Sophie.

Sophie Very well. Mr Ward . . . (*She inclines her head graciously*)

Richard bows slightly

Sophie exits up the stairs. Vivien comes down them and approaches Richard

Vivien It was very good of you, Mr Ward.

Richard To tell a lie to my host?

Vivien Why did you then?

Richard Why? Because I find myself sympathetic to your cause. I think that women should have the vote.

Vivien Is this a sudden conversion?

Richard I have been moving towards it for some time. Perhaps you will understand when I tell you that my aunt—my favourite aunt —is Lady Penelope Davey.

Vivien and Richard stay in frozen attitudes during the following

> *In the street. P.C. Dougan's obstinacy has increasingly exasperated Josiah. Now, angered beyond bearing, he rushes at the Constable with fist upraised to strike. Nathan flings himself between the two men, seizes Josiah and drags him away. Unruffled, P.C. Dougan draws back—unafraid but not wishing to provoke the Mayor-elect. He stands imperturbably stroking his whiskers. Lilian Malin comes through the arch. She pauses aghast when she sees her husband struggling with a police Inspector. Lilian is under fifty, neatly and quietly dressed, and she carries a Bible in her hand. Josiah ceases to struggle when he becomes aware of her. Nathan releases Josiah and the two men stand looking at her sheepishly. Then, with one accord, they rush over to her, point to P.C. Dougan and obviously present her with their view of the situation. The three remain in animated (though unheard) conversation with P.C. Dougan regarding them apprehensively*

Vivien I am honoured, Mr Ward, to meet a nephew of the woman who has been my idol ever since I joined the Women's Social and Political Union.

Richard Perhaps one day, Miss Malin, I shall be able to introduce you to her.

Vivien Oh, if you could! It would be the greatest experience of my life. And now I must go.

She reaches for the banister. Richard places a hand on hers

Richard Yes, but not before . . .

Vivien Before? (*Slowly, almost reluctantly, she withdraws her hand*)

Richard Before I tell you that the greatest experience of my life was meeting you—here in this room.

Vivien It was?

Richard (*gazing at her with adoration*) Yes—and for the rest of my life I shall regard you as the sweetest, most charming, gentlest girl I have ever met.

Vivien (*enchanted*) O-oh! (*She smiles, turns and, as if in a trance, begins to mount the stairs. Then turns to look back at him*) You did say the sweetest?

Richard I did

Still smiling, she turns and climbs one more stair before facing him again

Vivien And the gentlest? You did say the gentlest?

Richard That is what I said.

She sighs happily, resumes her ascent and this time does not pause or turn until she achieves the landing

Vivien I am most flattered but I think I ought to tell you ——

Richard Yes?

Vivien —that I am the one who bit the Inspector's thumb.

Vivien goes

Richard moves away from the foot of the stairs, to sit on the settee. He turns to direct a doubtful speculative glance towards the stairs. Then he sighs and relapses into a daydream which, from his expression, involves Vivien

In the street. Lilian has listened with growing indignation to the soundless but gesticulatory presentation of the case against P.C. Dougan. Obviously deeply influenced by what the men have to say, she raises her hand to indicate that she has had enough and she strides over to P.C. Dougan with Josiah and Nathan following. Pausing in front of him, she appears to address him spiritedly and her furious glances and finger pointed at the front door demonstrate that she is angry with Dougan for suggesting that her house might provide a sanctuary for suffragettes. Before the force of this assault, P.C. Dougan strives vainly to defend himself. He retreats, retreats again, and Lilian presses her attack with such vigour that he turns and flees.

Lilian expresses satisfaction in a separate nod for each of the men. Then she wheels about and goes into the house with Nathan and Josiah in close attendance.

Richard rises when he sees Lilian. Lilian pauses and looks a Josiah

Josiah Oh, this is Mr Ward, Lilian, who is to be the Liberal candidate. My wife, Lilian, Mr Ward.

Lilian offers her hand. Richard takes it and bows over it

Lilian A true Liberal is always welcome in this house, Mr Ward. (*To Nathan*) What is the matter with your hand, Inspector? I noticed you had . . .

Josiah He's been bitten. One of the women bit him.

Lilian Let me look at it.

Nathan goes to her, and she removes the bloody handkerchief

Yes, it's not too pleasant. You need a dressing on it. I won't be a moment. (*She goes to the door and then looks back at Josiah*) I think the Inspector ought to have a drink.

Lilian exits

Josiah She's right, you know. (*He picks up the decanter*) Drop of whisky, Nathan?

Nathan No, no. I'm on duty. I couldn't. I just couldn't. (*But he speaks in the tone of one already yielding to temptation and he is looking longingly at the decanter*)

Josiah Come, lad, You've had a shock to your system. I'm told that, in the tropics, they always prescribe whisky for snakebite.
Nathan A small one then.

Josiah pours and glances enquiringly at Richard

Josiah One for you?
Richard Not for me. I've had enough.
Josiah I'm relieved to hear it. I was beginning to think you hadn't got a limit. (*He does, however, pour another whisky*) I'll just have a nightcap. (*He picks up his glass and sips*) A wonderful woman, Lilian. She'll look after you, Nathan. She's as good as a doctor.
Nathan I've no doubt. No doubt at all.
Josiah Cooking, nursing, needlework, dressmaking, good works. . . . Yes, she's a rare woman, an exceptional woman. That's why I married her.

Lilian comes in carrying a tray upon which is a bowl of water, lint, a bandage and a pair of scissors. She goes over to the settee

Lilian If you'd bring that small table over here, Mr Ward.
Richard Yes, of course.

Richard picks up the small table and sets it in front of the settee. Lilian puts the tray on it

Lilian Thank you, Mr Ward. (*She sits on the settee*) Now, Inspector, if you'll sit there. . . . (*She pats the cushion beside her*)

Nathan sits as directed, taking off his cap and placing it, with his stick, on the floor beside him

What were you saying as I came in, Josiah?
Josiah (*rather embarrassed*) Why, that you're a Jill of all trades. That you can do anything you put your mind to.
Lilian I wish that was true. I can do most things that fall to a house-wife's lot—after a fashion. But it is a fact that I am comforter, nurse, hostess, accountant, secretary, laundress and seamstress in this establishment.
Nathan Very creditable, Mrs Malin.
Lilian And all without one penny of salary or wages.
Josiah Oh, come, Lilian, you know everything I have is yours.
Lilian Do you know that is absolutely true——

Josiah preens

—until I want something to wear or something for the house.
Josiah I'm not made of money, Lilian.
Lilian I'm not altogether sure what you're made of, Josiah. (*She takes Nathan's hand in hers and examines the bite*) You've got a wonderful set of teethmarks there. You've just got to find the girl who fits them. (*She bathes his hand with a piece of lint*)

Nathan I'll find her and, when I do, I'll put my stick to good use before I take her in. Ar-rrh! (*He wrenches his thumb away and covers it protectingly with his other hand*)

Lilian Too hot for you, Inspector?

Nathan Just a little.

Lilian It has to be hot if it's to do any good. (*She recovers his hand, bathes it more gently and proceeds to bandage it during the following*) Yours is a dangerous job, Inspector.

Nathan I never used to think so but since this suffragette menace started. It's not just the violence—(*He winces*)—it's the danger to property—the burning . . .

Lilian Ah, they're a determined lot. They'll stop at nothing.

Josiah It'll do them no good. They'll never get the vote by employing these methods. Never in this world!

Richard I wouldn't be too sure. The movement's growing. There's grave concern in Westminster—grave concern.

Josiah There may be. There may be concern in Westminster but Westminster isn't England by a long chalk, thank God! Look at the situation calmly—logically.

Richard Oh, I have done.

Josiah Well, then. Do you think the British Empire—the greatest empire in the world has ever known—is going to give way to a collection of screaming termagants?

Richard It's possible.

Josiah Eh?

Richard British Governments have never relished being laughed at and they might conceivably yield the point to avoid the world's ridicule.

Josiah I never heard such bloody nonsense in my life! Understand this! I shall have to speak for you at the adoption meeting next week and I'd be speaking against my conscience if I thought you were really serious. Just watch yourself, Mr Ward. I'm making allowances seeing that you're from the South.

Lilian There, Inspector. That should be all right for a little while.

Nathan Thank you, Mrs Malin. You're very kind.

Lilian It's the least we can do for one who is protecting us.

Nathan (*rising*) Ah, if only everybody was of your mind. I must be off.

Nathan starts for the front door with Josiah about to follow, but both men are halted by Lilian's next word

Lilian Inspector . . .

Nathan Yes?

Lilian I'm really concerned about you—out there on your own.

Nathan Oh, no need to be concerned, Mrs Malin. No need at all.

Lilian I'm not sure. (*She points to his hand*) That was *one* girl, Inspector. Suppose you were surrounded by a gang of them.

Nathan opens his mouth to issue a confident reassurance but is checked by Lilian's raised hand

It *could* happen. I wouldn't give much for your chances if you fell into their hands.

Nathan considers this and, before their eyes, changes from a confident man to one who is intimidated. Troubled, he starts from the hall, with Josiah following

Josiah Don't take on, Nathan. She didn't mean to upset you.

But Nathan shakes his head refusing comfort and does not speak until Josiah has opened the front door and he himself is in the street

Nathan She's right, you know. She's not wrong. A gang of women. If they were to surround you . . . (*He shudders*) A man wouldn't stand a dog's chance. Good night.
Josiah Good night, Nathan.

Lilian and Richard remain in frozen attitudes. Josiah stands ruminating in the hall

In the street. Minnie Brown, Nelly Brown's smaller, younger sister, comes through the arch and watches Nathan make a visible attempt to pull himself together. He draws himself to his full height, inflates his chest and there is the promise of a swagger in the experimental flourish of his stick. But, suddenly, he catches sight of Minnie and is immediately deflated and apprehensive. He turns and runs off R. *Minnie watches his departure, shrugs, shakes her head and goes back through the arch*

Josiah returns from the hall, picks up his glass and looks reflective. Lilian and Richard relax their attitudes

Lilian What do you think of the town, Mr Ward?
Richard I haven't been here very long but it strikes me as being very lively. The people I've met so far are splendid—industrious, frank and honest. It will be an honour to represent them in Parliament.
Lilian To represent them? The suffragettes, of course, would say that you are representing only the men of Metringham.
Josiah What's that? What did you say?
Lilian Mr Ward said it would be an honour to represent this town in Parliament.
Josiah Yes, yes. But what was it you said?
Lilian That the suffragettes would say he did not represent them— only the men of Metringham.
Josiah Then they would be talking a lot of claptrap! Of course he would be representing them. They live in Metringham and he would be M.P. for the borough, wouldn't he? They'll be able to consult him, to appeal to him, won't they?

Lilian Yes, but they could say they hadn't voted for him—that he wasn't their choice.

Josiah Why should they have a choice? Nobody's asking them. Nobody's consulting them. They haven't *got* a vote.

Lilian Exactly.

Josiah Here, what's this? My own wife in my own house! Are you agreeing with them? Supporting them? Because if you are . . .

Lilian No, no. Of course not. But I do think you should try to see what they are getting at—try to see their point of view.

Josiah Point of view? But they haven't got one. All they want is the vote. That's their parrot cry. And if they got it, do you know what? They wouldn't know what to do with it.

Richard I—I really ought to be going . . .

But the antagonists are at grips and his words go unheeded

Lilian That would have to be seen, wouldn't it?

Josiah It's a foregone conclusion. Women are emotional—easily influenced. They'd vote for the best-looking candidate and we'd have a Parliament of matinee idols without an idea in their heads.

Lilian Do you think they would be any worse than the present lot?

Josiah I don't know how you dare say that in front of our prospective candidate.

Lilian So sorry, Mr Ward. Nothing personal intended.

Josiah Now, Lilian, leave it alone. Don't provoke me further. I'm a patient man but you can go too far.

Lilian Ah, I see. Freedom of speech is suspended.

Josiah Never. Never in this house. You're free to say just what you like . . .

Lilian I am?

Josiah As long as you're sensible about it.

Lilian Who is to judge whether I am sensible or not? What you really mean is that I can say what I like ——

Josiah Yes?

Lilian —as long as I agree with you.

Josiah Now I never said anything of the sort. (*Turning to Richard*) Did I? Did I? I appeal to you, Mr Ward . . .

Richard I'm not sure that I am really qualified . . .

Josiah The plain fact is, Lilian, that you're just not fitted to understand politics. No woman is. It's just not in their—their composition.

Lilian It's true I haven't had your advantages.

Josiah If we gave way on this issue, it could lead to the downfall of the British Empire. There'd be developments. The suffragettes would see to that, wouldn't they, Mr Ward?

Richard I suppose they would. But I ought to be . . .

Josiah Can you see a woman as a Member of Parliament?

Lilian Of course.

Josiah Don't talk flaming nonsense! Could you imagine a woman in a Cabinet post?

Lilian Most certainly I could.

Josiah Then all I can say is: you've a better imagination than I have.

Lilian That could well be. That could well be.

Josiah You must see, Lilian, that the man has to make the decisions in matters of this sort. You have your own particular sphere of activity.

Lilian Where, presumably, I make the decisions. But I can't think of any I'm ever called upon to make.

Josiah Oh, I can. You chose the new curtains for our bedroom.

Lilian True.

Josiah And I left it to you to decide whether we went to Scarborough or Blackpool for the holidays.

Lilian All of which means that I have as much freewill as a backward child of ten.

Josiah Now, Lilian. Now—I've told you—you have your own particular sphere.

Lilian OO—oo—*ooh!*

It is a sound composed of humiliation, frustration and helpless rage and it startles both Josiah and Richard. Perplexed and frightened, they stare at her. Lilian glowers belligerently, ignoring them. Josiah braces himself to speak but relapses when Richard signals him to keep silent. All three stand staring directly ahead—the men obviously embarrassed. At length—

Josiah   It's no good going on . . .   *{ speaking*
Richard I'm afraid it's getting late . . . *together*
Josiah   I do beg your pardon. Please . . .   *{ speaking*
Richard I'm so sorry. Do go on.   *together*

There is no denying Josiah's gesture of polite insistence

Richard I was just observing that it is getting late and I ought . . .

Lilian Don't let me drive you away. I'm afraid I allowed myself to be provoked. Oh well, I'm sure you have many weighty matters to discuss.

Richard seems about to disagree

In any case, I'm going to bed. (*She offers her hand to Richard*)

Richard takes Lilian's hand

I hope you'll come and see us again soon.

Richard I shall be happy to do so. It has been a great pleasure to meet you, Mrs Malin.

Lilian prepares to leave, then pauses

Lilian Mr Ward . . .
Richard Yes?
Lilian Have you ever wished to be a character in history?

Richard looks to Josiah for enlightenment but finds none

A character with whom you were sympathetic and with whom you would wish to be identified—one who fulfilled his life as you would wish to fulfil yours . . .

Richard Why yes, Mrs Malin. Yes, I have. I would like to have been the younger Pitt.

Lilian The younger Pitt. One can see why. He was Prime Minister at twenty-five, wasn't he?

Richard At twenty-four.

Lilian Twenty-four . . . (*She makes for the stairs, ascends to the landing and looks back*) You disappoint me, Mr Ward. You might at least have enquired whether I had ever wished to be a character in history itself.

Richard I'm so sorry, Mrs Malin. With which character would you seek to identify yourself?

Lilian Soon answered, Mr Ward. (*She darts a venomous glance at Josiah*) Charlotte Corday.

Lilian inclines her head in dismissal and farewell, then turns, climbs the stairs and disappears from view

Josiah and Richard watch her exit as though mesmerized. Josiah turns from the stairs wearing an expression of shocked disbelief

Josiah Charlotte Corday? Wasn't she the one who . . .

Richard The one who stabbed Marat to death in his bath.

Josiah I don't know what's got into her. I've never known her like this. They're funny cattle, women. You can live with them, have children by them and never know what they really think. But you know what this is, don't you?

Richard What is it?

Josiah Reaction. Reaction, that's what it is. The result of suffragette agitation and activity. It's affecting all the women. They're getting rebellious—above themselves.

Richard That's only too evident. I'm gratified to note that you are coming round to my view of the seriousness of the suffragette challenge.

Josiah Don't gloat, lad. Don't gloat. Things have happened tonight to change my opinion. But I'm still of the same mind about the outcome—they'll fail because they haven't got a case.

Richard It's too late to begin another argument. I'll see you to-morrow at the Liberal Club.

Josiah At twelve o'clock sharp.

Richard I'll be off then.

Richard moves in the direction of the front door with Josiah following. Josiah opens the door. They shake hands on the threshold

Thank you for a most interesting evening, Mr Malin.

Josiah I'm sorry you had to witness the—the little difference of opinion.

Richard Oh, please . . .

Josiah You'll keep it to yourself, I'm sure.

Richard (*moving to the street*) Of course I will. Good night, Mr Malin.

Josiah (*calling after him*) Good night, Mr Ward. Be careful now. (*He closes the front door*)

> *Richard reaches the arch, looks back at the house, then passes through the arch and exits*

> *Josiah returns thoughtfully to the room where he reflectively picks up his glass as he glances towards the stairs*

I'm certain of one thing—I'll be sure to lock the door next time I have a bath.

The light goes out in the house

> *In the street. A drumbeat, measured and menacing, announces the advent of P.C. Thomas Dougan. He appears through the archway and paces slowly and ponderously around the exterior of the house and then turns smartly to retrace his steps. The drumbeats punctuate each measured stride and produce an effect of threat and suspense. Suddenly, he quickens his pace and, to the accompaniment of a stirring drum-roll, he rushes foward, halts to the R of the arch and, drawing himself up to his full height, points an accusing finger at the front door*

The street lighting fades to a Black-Out

CURTAIN

ACT II

SCENE 1

SCENE—*The following evening*

When the CURTAIN *rises, both house and street are empty. Above, Josiah is heard shouting: "Lilian! Lilian!" Then he comes clattering down the stairs. He is wearing black-braided trousers and a stiff-bosomed shirt which hangs out of his trousers. The collar is attached to the shirt by a back stud but has still to be fastened to the front stud. An untied black bow hangs round his neck. He calls out as he runs down the stairs.*

Josiah Lilian! Why don't you answer? (*He rushes over to the door, opens it and bawls*) Lilian! Come here and give us a hand! (*He waits and then wilts when there is no reply. Forlornly, he comes back into the middle of the room*) I thought she was here. (*Dispiritedly, he wanders over to the farthest bounds of the room where, on the "fourth wall", he apparently catches sight of himself in a mirror. He draws closer to it and tries to cope with his collar. After twisting his neck and pulling the collar, he manages to fasten one side. The other side proves more difficult but, after much pulling and twisting he finally achieves his objective. Sighing, he contemplates his reflection and sets about tying his bow. This proves to be an even more difficult operation than fastening the collar and he is continually unfastening his tie and starting again becoming more and more exasperated with each abortive attempt. At length, he achieves a parody of a bow and turns slowly left to right, right to left, as he stares dejectedly at his mirror image and shakes his head.*

Lilian, wearing indoor clothes, appears on the stairs

Lilian Were you calling?
Josiah Was I calling? I should think they heard me in Horsemarket Street. Look at me.
Lilian I am looking. Do I have to guess what you are supposed to be?
Josiah I can't get this blasted tie to behave.
Lilian I'm not surprised. To begin with, you fret yourself into such a state I marvel you can climb into your trousers unaided.
Josiah It's this stupid stiff shirt and this damned ridiculous tie.
Lilian I'm glad you said that. (*She descends the remaining stairs*) I'm glad you admit it's ridiculous. You men are quick to criticize women's clothes but what about yourselves?

Josiah What do you mean? There's nothing wrong with . . .

Lilian Isn't there? Look at the way you dress yourselves for what is supposed to be a festive occasion. When you're in all your finery, what do you most resemble? A flock of penguins.

Josiah We do not! Men look most distinguished in black and white, and they don't in the least look like a flock of penguins.

Lilian Don't they? They do to me—and I'm not alone in my opinion. Mind you, Mrs Marshall disagreed with me when I mentioned the penguin comparison at the last Ladies' Night.

Josiah I should think so! What did she say?

Lilian She said—now let me see—ah! She said you resembled nothing so much as a desolation of funeral mutes.

Josiah Very well. Very well. I've often wondered what you women talk about when you're giggling away together. Now I know. This may not be the ideal evening wear but it's just a bit late to change the fashion in time to be any use at this particular function. *Will you or will you not fasten this bloody tie?*

Lilian Who could refuse when you ask so nicely? If you'll stand perfectly still . . .

Josiah stands still, and she deftly ties the tie

There! That didn't hurt, did it? (*She pats the bow finally into place*) What do you say?

Josiah (*gruffly*) Thank you.

Lilian You look so miserable. Do you have to go to this affair to-night?

Josiah Of course. My position makes it necessary. This is a Liberal Party celebration.

Lilian Your position?

Josiah My position as Mayor-elect—as the leading Liberal in the town.

Lilian "The leading Liberal in the town." H'm—yes, I suppose some would so describe you.

Josiah Wouldn't you? Wouldn't you so describe me?

Lilian I should hesitate. (*She moves away to the foot of the stairs where she pauses*) Obviously my understanding of the word "Liberal" differs from yours. (*She ascends the stairs and turns on the landing to survey him*) And, Josiah . . .

Josiah Yes?

Lilian Please tuck your shirt in. From here you remind me of nothing so much as a frilled ham.

Lilian exits into the corridor. Josiah, speechless with rage, also goes up the stairs and disappears from view.

In the street. Richard appears through the arch. As he does so, the lights come up on the street. Richard approaches the front door, pauses to adjust his cravat, then knocks on the door resoundingly.

Vivien enters on the landing, trips down the stairs, runs and opens the front door, and drags Richard into the hall

Vivien They haven't gone yet. In here.

Still holding Richard by the hand, she drags him through the hall and out by the door, going out with him.
    After a moment Lilian appears on the stairs, now wearing coat and hat. As she reaches the foot, Vivien emerges from the door

Lilian Was that somebody at the door? (*She moves towards the fireplace*)
Vivien At the door?
Lilian Yes, I heard a knock.
Vivien Oh, there was somebody. (*She starts to climb the stairs*)
Lilian Who was it?
Vivien A man wanted to know the way to the Brocklehurst Museum.
Lilian At this time of night? The museum closes at six o'clock.
Vivien That's what I told him.

Vivien exits up the stairs

Lilian gazes after her doubtfully, then shrugs her shoulders and sits down

    After a moment Josiah hurtles into view on the stairs, wearing a silk hat, white silk scarf and dark overcoat. He glances wildly about the the room as he descends but fails to see Lilian. At the bottom of the stairs he turns and shouts

Josiah Come on, Lilian. I'm going to be late! Lilian!

As he is speaking, Lilian rises and glides over to where he is standing

Lilian Then let's go. I'm ready.

Josiah is very startled. He staggers, clutches his side and whirls to face her

Josiah Never do that again. Never do it again. It's enough to frighten anybody to death. I didn't know you were there.
Lilian Only because you didn't look. Imagine you being frightened of me.

Josiah totters to an armchair and sits to recover

Josiah It was the suddenness of it. You'd no right to come stealing up . . . (*He breathes deeply and then looks up*) Where did you say you were going?
Lilian You don't listen. To the Elmwood Mission Hall—a meeting of the Bible Tract Society.

Josiah It's on my way. We could walk along together. It always looks well—husband and wife out together.

Lilian And that's what you're concerned with, isn't it? Appearances.

Josiah Yes, it is. Anything wrong with that?

Lilian A great deal but we won't go into it now. Come on.

Josiah Will Vivien be all right? (*He rises*)

Lilian Of course. Sophie will be with her.

Josiah Oh, yes . . .

Lilian Come along. I'll be late.

Josiah leads the way to the front door, opens it and follows Lilian into the street

Josiah I'll leave you at the end of Millom Street.

Lilian There's no need for you to trouble yourself . . .

Josiah pauses and checks Lilian with upraised hand as if he is about to make an important announcement. He is:

Josiah You spoke just now as if this dinner was going to be a dull affair. I tell you it will be an occasion. After his election has been announced Winston Churchill is coming over to drink a victory toast with the loyal Liberals of Metringham. There! What do you think of that?

Lilian Are you quite sure he'll be drinking a victory toast?

Josiah I'm sure. Aren't you?

Lilian (*moving to the arch*) Not if all I hear is true.

Josiah That's the most disloyal speech I ever heard.

Lilian exits through the arch. Josiah follows. The lights fade on the street.

Sophie enters down the stairs. She goes to the door, opens it, and calls within

Sophie It's all right, Mr Ward. You can come out now.

Richard enters, looking apprehensive

Richard You're quite sure they've gone?

Sophie Quite sure. I watched them from my window. Vivien will be down in a minute.

Richard Thank you. It is good of you to be so—so sympathetic.

Sophie Oh, I am. Sympathetic and grateful—so very grateful for the way you helped all three of us last night.

Richard Really, it wasn't anything.

Sophie Oh, but it was. We could have been caught and so rendered useless to the Cause. We in the Movement are not yet accustomed to receiving assistance from men.

Richard Perhaps I am rather a special case. Miss Malin may have told you that my aunt is Lady Penelope Davey.

Sophie Indeed she has. Your behaviour is just what I would have expected from the nephew of such a devoted and dedicated woman.

Richard Yes?

Sophie Perhaps I'm speaking out of turn—maybe I am anticipating events—but you are interested in Vivien, aren't you?

Richard Very interested. My hope is that my interest is reciprocated.

Sophie She isn't a trivial girl, Mr Ward. She has high principles— firm resolve—and, when she commits herself, it will be for life. I wouldn't like to think—to think . . .

Richard To think that I would trifle with her affections.

Sophie There! You've said it for me. You're so helpful, Mr Ward. But then, it is no more than I would expect. I am so fond of her. So very fond.

Richard You don't have to worry, Miss Ormesby. My only concern is that she might possibly trifle with my affections.

Sophie Oh, I don't think you need trouble yourself on that score— not after what Vivien told me. I shouldn't have told you. I shouldn't have told you that. It's just that I trust you. You see, I recognized you.

Richard Recognized me? You said that last night. I don't think we've ever met before . . .

Sophie Before last night. Just the same, I recognized you at once. You would laugh if I told you why.

Richard Try me. Go on, try me.

Sophie You're the one I was told to wait for.

Richard Oh, yes . . .

Sophie And I waited—patiently and faithfully. We would have been perfect for each other. But something has gone wrong. There's been a slip in time somewhere.

Richard There has?

Sophie So I can only step aside and wish you all happiness. In the circumstances, you couldn't do better than Vivien. She's a dear, sweet girl. (*She reaches out and gently strokes his cheek*) My blessing on you both.

Sophie turns from him and begins to mount the stairs. He stands quite still watching her fixedly. She pauses and looks back

You're not . . . not laughing at me?

Richard No, I wouldn't ever laugh at you.

Sophie I knew you at once but I couldn't speak then—especially when I saw that you hadn't recognized me. Time was against us.

Sophie exits up the stairs

Richard, deeply disturbed, moves slowly to an armchair and sits, wearing a shocked expression

Vivien enters down the stairs

Vivien What's the matter?

Richard rises

Have you seen a ghost?

Richard In a manner of speaking, yes.

Vivien It's Cousin Sophie, isn't it? What has she been saying to you?

Richard Well it's a little difficult to be specific.

Vivien You can tell me. I'm used to her. She is sometimes a little strange but she doesn't mean any harm. I told Mother about it but she says it's her age. I do hope she didn't embarrass you.

Richard No—I don't embarrass easily. She is obviously a dear, sweet lady and quite devoted to you.

Vivien What did she say? What did she say about me?

Richard If you really want to know . . .

Vivien I do! I do!

Richard She said I was originally predestined to mate with her——

Vivien Oh, no!

Richard —but as there had been some error in the time-scale, I could do a lot worse than marry you.

Vivien Oh, how dreadful! How shaming! I can't look you in the face. (*But doing so just the same*) What did you say?

Richard The only thing possible—I agreed with her. But I can't think that you invited me here to discuss your cousin. Or did you?

Vivien Of course not. It was about—about last night. I didn't want you to be under any misapprehension. Please understand that I am a sincere and committed suffragette and any—any relationship between us must recognize this fact. But perhaps I take too much for granted. Perhaps you didn't mean . . .

Richard But I did. I do. I want you to be my wife. I'll make you a formal proposal of marriage if you like.

Vivien You'll have gathered that I am not one for formality. But I would like a proposal—that is, if you could manage one at short notice.

Richard Will this do? I love you, Vivien. Will you marry me?

Vivien Yes, Richard. Gladly and willingly.

Richard takes her in his arms and kisses her

(*After a moment, freeing herself*) There's nothing like informality, is there, Richard? (*And to prove it, she kisses him again*)

At length, they separate

Can I trust you?

Richard (*offended*) If you can't, then you've just made a singularly bad choice of a husband.

Vivien No, no. It's something concerning the Women's Social and Political Union. I don't know whether I ought to tell you—with you being the Liberal candidate.

Richard If you have been looking forward to being the wife of the Member for Metringham, then I have a disappointment for you: I do not think that the principles of Liberalism are truly practised in Metringham and I intend to send in my resignation as prospective candidate.

Vivien Oh, Richard, how splendid!

Richard You're pleased?

Vivien I'm delighted! Ecstatic! I'll tell you my news at once. This was the second thing I wanted to tell you.

Richard Well, what is it?

Vivien I'm running away from home—tonight.

Richard Running away? Whatever for?

Vivien I am one of two suffragettes selected to go to London to join the Headquarters staff of the Women's Social and Political Union.

Richard But what about your mother and father? What are you going to tell them?

Vivien I've written a note and I'll write again—to my mother—when I get to London.

Richard It hardly seems fair . . .

Vivien Fair! You know something of my father by now. Is he fair? Is he just? Is he even humane where women are concerned? Don't trouble to answer. I'm surprised my mother didn't leave him years ago. After the meeting here . . .

Richard Oh, there's to be a meeting here.

Vivien Yes, but you're not supposed to know—a meeting of our executive committee is to be addressed by one of the leading officers of the W.S.P.U. She's quite a formidable person, I understand.

Richard I'm sure she is. But you said, "After the meeting here . . ."

Vivien Oh yes. After the meeting, I'm going to the station to catch the night train to London.

Richard Are you? I'm not having you going up to London on your own . . .

Vivien Richard! You're not to dictate to me.

Richard I'm not having you going up to London by yourself—so I shall come with you.

Vivien You wonderful! Aren't you the kindest, sweetest, most considerate person!

Richard And that isn't all. How old are you, Vivien?

Vivien Twenty-one last January.

Richard That decides it. You shall stay with my Aunt Penelope.

Vivien With Lady Penelope Davey? Oh, bliss! Oh, Heaven!

Richard But only for a day or two. We shall be married as soon as I can get a special licence.

Vivien Married? So soon?

Richard Would you like to wait? Am I being impetuous?

Vivien Oh, I like you to be impetuous. But I thought we'd have to wait. A special licence! Are you rich, Richard?

Richard Shall we say that I have a modest competence?

Vivien (*wheedling*) Richard . . .

Richard I shall not reveal anything further respecting my financial position because I don't want to think that you are marrying me for my money.

Vivien Oh, but, Richard, I should, if possible, love you even more if you were rich. I've always dreamed of marrying a rich man. Shall we have a motor car?

Richard I already have two motor cars.

Vivien Oh, I do hope I don't wake up. Not just yet. You'll have to go. They'll be here for the meeting. Where shall I see you?

Richard On the platform. Look out for me. I'll try for a reserved compartment.

Vivien But what about the others?

Richard What others?

Vivien The other suffragettes. We're all supposed to be travelling together.

Richard Well, you're not. You'll just have to tell them, won't you?

Vivien (*embracing him*) Oh, aren't you masterful? I can see I'm going to have a terrible time.

They kiss

Where are you going now? Just so I can think of you.

Richard If you must know, I'm going to the Liberal Club.

Vivien But I thought you said . . .

Richard I'm going to write a letter of resignation which I shall address to your father. After all, there are certain formalities to be observed.

Vivien Poor Father! He's going to get some rather disturbing correspondence, isn't he? (*Suddenly urgent*) You'll really have to go. I don't want to have to explain you to Captain Ada Leyland.

Richard Who on earth is she?

Vivien I told you—the leading official of the W.S.P.U. who is coming to address us tonight.

Richard Oh, yes. I'll be off.

He holds out his arms. She rushes to him and they kiss protractedly. When they separate, they are dazed and shaken. They stand looking at each other surprised and shocked by their shared desire

In the street. The lights come up. Through the arch comes Lady Honoria Cumberleigh and Eulalia (Moppet) Powle. Honoria is about forty-five and is heavily built. Her decidedly masculine appearance is heightened by one or two male touches: a mannish hat, a suit of mannish cut, and a blouse closely resembling a shirt which is topped by a collar and bow tie. Eulalia is in her twenties—dainty, very feminine and possessed of an affected voice and posture. They contemplate the house

Richard backs slowly in the direction of the hall with Vivien following at the same time. There is about them now an atmosphere of mutual fatal attraction and clearly they are in imminent danger of yielding to it. Richard reaches the front door, flings it open and reaches the safety of the street. Vivien stands regarding the door for a moment or two and then returns to the room where she sinks into an armchair and sits staring into her future

In the street. Richard closes the door behind him and backs towards the arch with his eyes hypnotically fixed on the front door

Eulalia A man! A man leaving the house!

The two women give way on either side of Richard as he approaches them. Honoria glares at him with marked disfavour but Eulalia, interested, intrigued and curious regards him with a bright and questing eye. As he passes, Honoria spits out

Honoria A man! Vile, cheating, false, faithless, perfidious, perjured, tyrannical, treacherous, fraudulent, double-dealing creature!

But, deaf to her words and blind to their presence, Richard moves on his tranced way towards the arch and then passes through it with Eulalia now pursuing him with a stalking motion.
Honoria watches her with mounting irritation and suspicion. Eulalia stands just short of the arch, peering beyond it and smiling

Moppet! *Mop-pet!* (*Exasperated when there is no response, and thundering*) Eulalia!

Eulalia turns with exaggerated innocence in both voice and expression

Eulalia Why, Bunty-dear, I was only looking!

Honoria "Only looking!" We know where that can lead to—next thing you know, you'd be involved. Involved! And what would happen then? What would happen?

Eulalia But, Bunty-darling, there's no danger. Nothing *can* happen. Great big you is here to protect me.

Honoria Suppose I wasn't—what would you do then?

Eulalia I wouldn't even stop to look. I'd be so frightened. I'd run and run until I got home—to you, Bunty.

Honoria Dear Moppet! Sometimes I think you mean it.

Eulalia But I do! I do! (*Becoming tearful*) You've got to trust me, Bunty. You've got to!

Honoria Oh, all right. *All right!* Don't blubber, child. And remember —no "Bunty" and no "Moppet" once we get inside. This is a serious business. (*She turns to the front door*)

Eulalia Oh, yes. Very serious indeed. I shall address you throughout as Madam Chairman, Honoria or Lady Cumberleigh. Oh, I shall be most circumspect and very respectful.

But Honoria is not listening—she is regarding the front door with speculation

Honoria This house—the home of the despicable Alderman Josiah Malin. What is it like? What shall we find when we pass within? A frowsty hall with a deplorable hatstand and then—God help us!—the utterly undistinguished drawing-room with a few poor pictures, a sagging settee, some uncomfortable armchairs, a sideboard executed in the worst possible taste and a truly hideous flight of stairs leading, let us hope and pray, to some slightly more attractive apartments above.

Eulalia But that's what it's like. That's exactly what it's like. Oh, aren't you a clever Bunty to guess what it's like inside.

Honoria Don't be a bloody stupid Moppet! I've been here before. (*And she gives three swift, sharp knocks on the door*)

Eulalia Oh, you called me Moppet—and you said we weren't to use pet-names.

Honoria I said "once we were inside". Do, for Heaven's sake, pay attention to what I say. (*And again she knocks thrice on the knocker*)

Eulalia Oh, aren't you stern and dominating!

In the house. Nelly emerges from the door. She sees Vivien and goes over to her

Nelly They're here, Miss Vivien.

Vivien takes no notice and continues to stare ahead wearing a blissful expression. The measured knocking is repeated as Honoria bangs away. There is no reaction from Vivien

I'll go and let them in. (*She moves towards the front door*)

In the Street. Rachel Randall comes hurrying through the arch. She is wearing a shabby travelling cape and is carrying a suitcase and a folder

Rachel Oh, I'm not late, am I?

Honoria No, no. We've just arrived.

Nelly opens the door, and greetings are exchanged as the three women pass into the hall and follow her into the room, Rachel sets down her suitcase in the hall

Sophie enters down the stairs, pausing at the foot

The three women group themselves round Vivien and regard her speculatively. She remains rapt

Vivien!

Vivien sits unheeeding. Honoria roars

Vivien!

Startled, Vivien leaps to her feet.

Vivien Yes, yes. What is it?

Honoria We'll get nowhere mooning and daydreaming, girl. Pull yourself together. We'll have Captain Ada Leyland here at any moment.

Sophie I have yet to meet this lady. What is she like?

Honoria I consider myself not easily impressed but, frankly, she intimidates me and, if I were a member of the present Government, she would terrify me to death. Come, let us arrange ourselves. Move this (*indicating the armchair*) over there.

Honoria indicates a spot more in line with the settee and Vivien and Nelly hasten to obey

Rachel, bring that chair here.

Rachel brings up the chair from beside the sideboard and the new arrangement makes a rough semicircle of settee and chairs. She then takes an exercise book and papers from her folder

Now the other armchair—beside this one.

Again Vivien and Nelly carry out the order bringing the remaining armchair to a position L *of the other chairs*

Sophia, Eulalia and Vivien on the settee

They sit as directed

You, Rachel, as secretary, on the straight-backed chair.

Rachel seats herself

I, as Chairwoman, will accommodate myself here. (*She eases herself into the armchair* R *of Rachel*) And you, Nelly . . .

Nelly Yes, Lady Honoria?

Honoria I want you to remain standing as a sort of sentry. Should anybody knock at the door after the meeting starts, count ten slowly, then go and open it. You will be quite safe because, by then, we shall have left by the back door. Understood, everybody?

There is a murmur of assent and Nelly takes up a position L *of Rachel. Honoria glances at the other armchair*

She can sit there and form her own opinion of how the Metringham branch conducts its business.

Rachel And what do we do now?

Honoria We wait. We wait for Captain Ada Leyland.

And they compose themselves into attitudes of waiting. But not for long

In the street. There is a dramatic drum-roll which heralds the advent of Captain Ada Leyland as she marches through the arch to her objective—the front door. The Captain is a woman of under forty, severely, but tastefully, dressed in a coat-frock of decidedly military cut with some enlivening touches of trimming and buttons. But she is not masculine—she is a very determined woman with about her something of the air associated with women lion-tamers. She halts, looks L (single drum stroke) and R (another single drum stroke), before seizing the knocker to rap out the necessary three swift knocks. For three beats she pauses and raps out three more swift knocks. Then she stands waiting

All the suffragettes rise uneasily

That's her. Let her in, Nelly. But see she gives the password.

Nelly goes to the front door as the others stand looking apprehensive

Ada I am expected. You know who I am.

Ada moves as if to enter but Nelly checks her with raised hand

Nelly Yes, I know. But first the password.
Ada Quite right, girl. It is Emmeline.

Ada strides into the hall. Nelly closes the door and follows her

Nelly Straight ahead, Captain Leyland.

All the waiting women stiffen into the position of attention. Once inside the room, Ada pauses and looks them over with the eye of an inspecting officer. They remain briefly in this position

In the street. P.C. Thomas Dougan appears under the arch. He is regarding the front door with a knowing air which suggests that he has Ada "under observation". The light in the street begins to fade but, before it goes out completely, it blazes on the face of the policeman. He smiles in gloating fashion: everything is going as he expected and soon he will be ready to pounce. The street lighting fades to a Black-Out

Ada Good evening, ladies.

Somebody sighs. The tension eases—they relax

All Good evening, Captain Leyland.
Honoria Captain Leyland, we are deeply honoured by your presence here tonight and we would ask you to honour us further by presiding over our executive Committee meeting.
Ada That I will gladly do. (*She sweeps them with a comprehensive glance*) Do you know why they call me Captain?
Rachel I don't know.

Vivien Nor I.

Ada We have at Headquarters General Flora Drummond. I serve her as executant of her strategy, as an instrument, as a weapon. But tonight I am here as deputy for Christabel Pankhurst who is in Manchester to lead this campaign in which you have taken part.

Honoria We should have achieved nothing without her.

Ada This branch of yours has particularly commended itself to Mrs Pankhurst for its efficiency—that is why I am taking two of your members back to London with me. You have done great work in helping our sisters in Manchester to bring down that so-called Liberal, Winston Churchill.

Rachel We have done our best, Captain Leyland.

Ada You have done well. Your leaders, Lady Honoria and Hippolyta, rank first among provincial commanders of our movement.

Sophie We don't know who Hippolyta is.

Ada She will make herself known in due course. Lady Honoria knows her.

Eulalia (*in her spoilt-child voice*) But Bunty won't tell anybody—not even her Moppet.

There is some embarrassment. Eulalia quails before Honoria's furious glance. Ada takes in the situation at a glance and acts to relieve the tension

Ada Perhaps we should begin the formal business of the meeting.

Honoria Yes, indeed. Take your places, please.

The committee members move towards their appointed places. Honoria indicates with a wave of the hand the armchair reserved for Ada. The committee members stand until Ada is seated and then they, too, sit. Ada notices that Nelly is still standing

Ada No chair for you, my girl?

Nelly If you please, Captain Leyland, I'm a sort of sentry and I know the house.

Ada Very well. Proceed.

Honoria The meeting is now in session. (*To Rachel*) Minutes and report later. Start with apologies.

Rachel Very well. Apologies for absence have been received from Mesdames Hughes, Hackney and Leacock. They, with many of our members, are waiting for the result in North Manchester.

Honoria We—we usually open our proceedings with a song written by one of our members.

Ada Then do so. I want nothing changed because I am present.

Honoria If you please, Rachel . . .

Rachel rises and moves to a central position. She sings the song with moving sincerity and her few—but telling—gestures serve to heighten the effect of the words

Rachel (*singing*) Is this the land?

> Is this the land where men walk free?
> Is this the land of liberty?
>
> Is this the land?
>
> Is this the land which claims to be
> The cradle of democracy?
>
> This is the land.
>
> This is the land where you will see
> Women live in slavery.
> This is the land, the land that we
> Will change for our posterity.
>
> This is the land.
>
> Through the night, sister, through the night,
> Through the night of tyranny!
> To the fight, sister, to the fight!
> Take my hand and come with me!
>
> O come with me and have no fear!
> The time is now! The hour is here!
>
> O come with me!

There is some applause and the song ends. Ada rises

Ada Thank you, my dear. You shall sing that song for us in London. Did you write it?

Rachel No. Sophie Ormesby wrote it. She writes all our songs.

Sophie rises and looks towards Ada appealingly

Ada We can make good use of your songs, Miss Ormesby—if all of them are of that quality.

Sophie Take me with the others. Take me with you to London.

Ada It is not yet time. Besides, there is work for you to do here.

Honoria Order! Order! Order, please! We shall never finish at this rate.

Sophie I should like to go to London. There is nothing to keep me here.

Honoria If you please, Sophie!

Reluctantly, Sophie resumes her seat

Now, Rachel, if you would read the minutes and make your report . . .

Rachel (*reading from her book*) Minutes of a meeting held on the sixteenth April, nineteen hundred and eight, at Marley Manor House.

Honoria (*to Ada*) My place.

Ada nods

Rachel In the Chair, Lady Honoria Cumberleigh; present the full Committee except for Miss Ormesby who was present part-time.

Sophie I was setting fire to the Co-operative Stores.

Ada What a splendid idea!

Honoria Not that we have anything against the Co-operative Movement, but the store is centrally situated and it was felt that a spectacular blaze in the heart of the town . . .

Ada Yes, yes—it was bound to draw attention to our cause.

Sophie They had it under control in half an hour.

Ada No matter—as long as they realized it was our work.

Rachel The Committee reviewed the results of our efforts in North Manchester where this branch is working in support of the Manchester W.S.P.U. in an attempt to prevent the election to Parliament of the Right Honourable Winston Churchill, President of the Board of Trade. The Chairwoman asked for it to be set on record that neither we nor our sisters in Manchester have any personal animosity against Mr Churchill but we are determined to show the Government that the militant suffragettes are a force to be reckoned with and they would do well to give us a hearing.

Ada True. They will have to treat with us sooner or later.

Rachel It was agreed, after some discussion, to continue our part of the campaign and on the same general lines of harassment and interruption adapting our tactics to the conditions prevailing.

They all look at Ada. Obviously, some comment is expected

Ada It strikes me as a very sensible procedure. There is, I gather, a report.

Rachel Yes. I will read it. The branch took part, during the past seven days, in interruptions at twelve open-air meetings and eight indoor meetings. At all of these we created the maximum disturbance, rising one by one at widely separated points and shouting slogans until we were ejected. Our Chairman achieved the most outstanding uproar when she was forcibly expelled from the Gladstone on the evening of eighteenth April.

Honoria I was frog-marched! Me, frog-marched! (*She rises excitedly*) But I called out (*shouting at the top of her voice*) "Down with male brutality! Votes for Women! Give us the Vote!"

The others regard her with alarmed expressions

(*Subsiding suddenly*) I'm sorry. I got carried away.

Ada (*to Nelly*) Just take a look outside and see that all is quiet.

Nelly At once, Captain Leyland.

Nelly goes to the hall. There is a brief silence

Honoria However, I did hit a steward and make his nose bleed.

Nelly opens the front door and glances from L to R. Satisfied, she closes the door. For a moment or two, she lingers in the hall and the suffragettes remain frozen in listening attitudes

In the street. The light above the arch comes on to reveal P.C. Thomas Dougan standing below it. He is watchful, implacable. When his presence has been established, the light fades and it is dark again in the street

The suffragettes relax as Nelly returns

Nelly All quiet in the street, Captain Leyland.
Ada Good. Thank you. But you can't be too careful. (*Turning to Rachel*) Where do you keep your reports?
Honoria In the safe at my place. She comes there to write up her minutes and reports—we're preserving them as historic documents.
Ada Burn them.
Honoria What? What did you say?
Ada Burn them. Report only from meeting to meeting. They would provide incriminating evidence if the police were to search your house.
Honoria Very well. We'll burn them. (*She sighs*) But it will be a great loss to posterity.
Ada Does that conclude the report?
Rachel Not quite. There have been other activities worthy of record: the mass attack on the postal services of the town resulting in the firing of thirty-two pillar-boxes on the night of the twenty-third of April.
Ada Yes, I heard of that. Very creditable.
Rachel There was a major event on the same night when we set fire to the Mechanics' Hall.
Honoria (*beaming on Sophie*) That was the work of Miss Sophie Ormesby who is our arson specialist.
Sophie (*sadly shaking her head*) But they had the blaze under control in just over twenty minutes.
Eulalia Never mind, dear. It's the thought that counts.
Rachel That concludes the report. Miss Hackney, as you know, is in North Manchester . . .
Ada Which is where you would all be if I hadn't asked you to hold your Committee meeting here tonight. I had special reasons for doing so as I shall presently explain.
Honoria Is there a pen? Then I can sign the report and minutes . . .

Nelly hastens to bring a pen and ink from the sideboard. Rachel passes the report and minute book to Honoria who signs both with a flourish

Rachel There doesn't seem much point in signing the minutes if we're going to burn them.

Honoria Procedure must be observed. (*She places the book and papers on the floor beside her and then rises*) This is the last time you will act as secretary of our meetings, Rachel, and I would like to thank you both for myself and on behalf of us all for your devoted service—rendered often under conditions of great difficulty.

All Hear, hear!

Honoria We shall miss you and we shall miss you, Vivien, for the youth, the enthusiasm and the fire which you brought to our cause. (*She takes two tiny parcels from her pocket*) Take this, Rachel.

Rachel takes the offering

And this, Vivien.

Vivien rises and also takes the proffered parcel

Inside each parcel is a watch which has been subscribed for by all our members. There is also a little money from me which will be useful to you in London.

As Rachel and Vivien are clearly about to express their thanks, she raises her hand

No. No, thanks. I find thanks very disturbing and I don't want to blub.

Rachel Just the same, we are grateful. Very grateful.

Vivien We are indeed—and we shall always remember you.

Honoria Yes, yes. Always remember us. Keep in touch. Write to us. Let us know how you are getting on.

Ada (*consulting a watch pinned to the bosom of her coat*) The result should be announced any time now.

Nelly Then we'll hear soon, Captain Leyland. My sister, Minnie, will come straight from the Town Hall.

Ada We'll do better than that. I gave Christabel Pankhurst this telephone number. She'll ring me up here.

Vivien Oh, dear! Will that—will that be all right?

Ada Of course it will. Have courage, girl. You'll have to learn to operate under the very noses of your enemies. Now then. I would like to take the measure of the two women who will be joining us at Headquarters. Your individual responses will help me to place you in the organization. Mrs Randall . . .

Rachel I'm not sure that I can . . .

Ada You can. Tell me why you are willing to leave home—your degree of dedication to the Cause . . .

Rachel Very well. I was the only child of a mill-owner. When he died, his business was sold and I found myself something of an heiress.

Because I could not help myself, I married Reuben Randall who is a wastrel, drunkard and gambler. (*She is struggling against tears of vexation and grief*)

Sophie goes to Rachel

Sophie Stop now if it upsets you.

Rachel disengages herself from Sophie but accepts her handkerchief with which she dries her eyes

Rachel No, no. I'll finish it now that I've started. He spent all my money in no time at all and since then we've lived in debt and on charity. I married him in hopes of changing him but he's changed me. I was a happy, hopeful person and I have become a scold, a drudge and, like him, a failure.

Honoria Not to us, Rachel. You're not a failure to us.

Rachel So you see the Cause means everything to me. It has to take the place of the hope, the home, the happiness and the children denied to me. The Cause is my dream and my life-work. Is that what you wanted?

Ada It is just what I wanted.

Rachel sits

I also left a husband. Mine knew himself to be omnipotent. On one of his bad days he merely believed himself to be first cousin of God. On his good days . . . (*She raises her eyes and shakes her head*) Miss Malin, let me hear from you.

Vivien (*rising*) I, too, am an only child. My father, as you know, is a local Liberal politician. He is narrow and bigoted in his views and irritating in his expression of them. He is a sworn opponent of women's suffrage and I have found it increasingly difficult to dissemble my true feelings and live in the same house with him. For these reasons I would be glad to leave home, to come to London and work for the Cause. But there is something else.

Ada Yes?

Vivien Today I have received a proposal of marriage which I have accepted.

Honoria (*rising wrathfully*) You intend to marry? To marry a man? A *man*?

Ada That is what I understood her to say. Are you about to propose an alternative?

Honoria No—no. I—I wasn't. (*Recovering*) But I don't trust any of them. All men are liars, schemers, brutes, criminals, scum of the earth . . .

Ada Yes, yes. But I'd like to hear more of the particular man. Who is he? What is he?

Vivien His name is Richard Ward and he was prospective candidate for this town. He has resigned because he does not believe that Liberal policy is truly interpreted here.

Ada Ah!

Honoria I don't believe him. I wouldn't believe him if he swore on a stack of Bibles. They're all . . .

Ada I know—liars, schemers and all the rest of it. But there *are* some men who are sympathetic to our cause. For instance, there was Dr Pankhurst and there's Mr Pethick-Lawrence . . .

Vivien He is in close sympathy with his aunt. You may have heard of her. She is Lady Penelope Davey.

The announcement makes a general impression

Ada There! Do you need any further reference?

Honoria She should have said that at first.

The telephone rings. All except Ada regard it apprehensively. She strides over to the instrument and picks it up. When she speaks, it is in a curiously measured "telephone" voice

Ada Hel-lo. Hel-lo. Who—is—it? . . . Oh,—it—is—you, Chris—ta —bel.

The others react to the name

What—did—you—say? . . . I—cannot—hear—you. There— seems—to—be—a—lot—of—dis—turb—ance. I said . . . (*Suddenly switching to her normal voice*) He did? How many? . . . Oh, how wonderful! How truly splendid! . . . Yes, yes. I'll tell them. Congratulations! Oh, congratulations! This is a great day! I'll see you at the station.

Shining-eyed, Ada hangs up. The others are waiting breathlessly for her to speak but she is wrapped in a dream of future successes. Indeed, she stands like a monument to Victory

Honoria (*shouting*) For the love of Heaven, what has happened?

Ada (*coming to earth*) Oh, my dears, I'm sorry. We've won—won handsomely. Winston Churchill has been defeated by five hundred and twenty-nine votes and——

They all express their delight noisily but are silenced when Ada raises her hand and shouts

—and both the successful candidate and the loser acknowledge the fact that the activities of the suffragettes had a marked effect on the result. We have today won a great victory.

There is further loud rejoicing which Ada makes no effort to suppress. She is again caught up in her dream of the future—a separate, detached and wholly fulfilled person. At length, she is brought back to the present by Eulalia and Vivien performing a ridiculous dance close to her

Now, now. Please—please . . .

They stand quiet and still—and looking at her

D

We have not much time and I have still to tell you the main purpose of my visit. Sit down and listen to me.

Obediently, they sit and Ada surveys them

I look at you and I see you as representative women forced to live in a man-made world, women denied the right to have any share in the government of their country, women who, however intelligent, are denied that which is freely available to dim-witted louts barely able to write their names and whose only qualification to vote is that they are male.

Sophie Tell us what we must do to change this!

Rachel Yes, tell us. Tell us!

Ada You shall have your opportunity sooner than you think. While the memory of our victory in North Manchester is still fresh in public memory, we shall strike again. We shall strike here in Metringham. You helped the women of North Manchester. They will help you to mount a campaign that will be memorable in our history. Details will be passed to Lady Honoria and Hippolyta.

Eulalia When? When will this be?

Ada Soon—very soon if it is to be effective.

Rachel Then couldn't we stay and take part?

Ada You place me in a position of some delicacy. You promise to respect my confidence?

All Yes. Oh, yes. Yes, indeed.

Ada It is just that Alderman Malin is to be one of the targets of the campaign so I feel it would be better . . .

Vivien I understand—better if I am not here.

Ada Precisely. Now here is the message I bring from our leader, Mrs Pankhurst: we shall increase the scope and range of our acts of militancy. We shall launch our attacks on the haunts of power and the seats of the mighty. We can expect a swift reaction from the Government. We face a long and bitter struggle during which we shall be called upon to suffer the certainty of violence and harsher prison sentences. Think of these things. If you feel you cannot face them, then I urge you to leave the movement. This is no time for the timorous or faint-hearted.

In the street. The light comes on. Lilian comes quickly through the arch on her way to the front door. During the following speeches, she opens the front door, strides into the room and stands regarding them

Honoria There is nobody faint-hearted or timorous in this branch.

Eulalia They'll not stop us by sending us to prison.

Honoria And we're not to be intimidated by violence.

Those seated rise. They regard Lilian with surprise and fear

Nelly It's not my fault, Lady Honoria. She let herself in with her key.

Vivien I don't know what to say to you, Mother.
Lilian I know what to say to you—Emmeline.
Honoria This is Hippolyta.

On their surprise, the light fades in both street and house

CURTAIN

SCENE 2

A few minutes later.

When the CURTAIN *rises, the suffragettes are all gathered as at the end of the previous scene. The stage is in darkness, but immediately a spot comes up on Lilian*

Lilian What is the greatest single force halting the march of progress? The race of men. As creatures men are no more civilized than they were two thousand years ago. There is still in them the same cruelty and indifference which allows them to tolerate crucifixion, wars, famine, epidemics, illiteracy, prostitution, slum housing and bad working conditions.

Light is becoming more general in the room now: a faint glow at first illuminating the listening suffragettes and then, as the general lighting grows in strength, the spotlight fades

These are evils which women feel deeply, personally, emotionally, and they will only cease to trouble us when women have a share in running the affairs of the world. But first we need the vote—the vote for us is the first step to a more humane, a safer, saner world.

Minnie enters in the darkness of the street and goes to the front door

Honoria The vote! We shall get it though it cost our lives!
Ada And if it means fighting for all our lifetimes.

Three thunderous knocks on the front door freeze them all into startled immobility

Lilian Wait . . .

She holds up her hand and, tense and still, they wait. Three more knocks resound through the house

Nelly It'll be our Minnie.

In the street. Light comes on to confirm that Minnie is on the threshold dancing with impatience

Lilian Let her in—and tell her that she overdid the pause.

Nelly speeds to the front door and opens it

Minnie We've won! We've won! And I came back in a motor car! (*She thrusts Nelly aside and rushes past her into the room shouting*) We've won! We've won by five hundred and twenty-nine votes . . . (*Her voice is fading and her enthusiasm visibly drains away as she senses a lack of response in her audience*) Oh, you know. Ah-h! Oh, dear! (*She has just noticed Lilian and registers shock and distress*)

Lilian It's all right, Minnie. I am one of you. I am Hippolyta.

Minnie Oh, thank Heaven. My heart stopped.

Lilian And this is Captain Ada Leyland.

Minnie aims a little bob in Ada's direction

She heard the result over the telephone. But you are an eye-witness. You tell us what you saw.

Minnie Then you don't know what Mr Joynson Hicks said after he'd won?

There is a general shaking of heads

Watch this then. (*She inflates herself in imitation of a successful candidate*) "I acknowledge the assistance I have received from those ladies who are sometimes laughed at but who, I think, will now be feared by Mr Churchill—the suffragettes."

Ada This is a triumph! A positive triumph!

Minnie wears a miserable expression

Lilian It is indeed—the public acknowledgement of our efforts. (*She notices Minnie*) But you don't look very happy, Minnie.

Minnie Mrs Malin, I'm not. I saw him. I heard him. Mr Churchill, I mean. He was pale but not—not cast down. He's a fine man, a great man, and we pushed him out. (*Faltering and near to tears*) I'm not sure we've done right.

Honoria (*going over to her*) Put your trust in God, Minnie—*She* will protect you.

Honoria moves away, leaving Minnie uncomforted

Ada There is no doubt that Winston Churchill is a great man and a magnanimous one. The morning after the disturbance at the Free Trade Hall, he went to the police station and offered to pay the fines for Christabel Pankhurst and Annie Kenney—he said he didn't want them to go to prison.

Rachel Wouldn't they let him pay the fines?

Ada Somebody else had already paid them. We have friends in unexpected places.

Minnie To offer to pay their fines when they had been arrested for interrupting his meeting! (*She becomes suddenly tearful*) We've done wrong and we shall never be forgiven!

Ada I don't think you need worry about Mr Churchill. Christabel told me that, seven minutes after the result was announced, he was offered the Liberal candidature in Dundee. Dundee is an impregnable Liberal stronghold. We couldn't hope to defeat him there.

Minnie (*drying her eyes*) You mean he's all right?

Lilian Of course he is. Winston Churchill is indestructible.

Ada (*looking at her watch*) Time to go. I have things to do before I meet you ladies at the railway station.

Sophie (*with sudden urgency*) Please take me. Take me with you to London.

Ada It isn't possible—yet. Besides, you still have things to do

Sophie (*reflecting*) Yes, you're right. Things to do—I have things to do.

Honoria We must go. The back way, Nelly, if you will lead the way.

Nelly Follow me, ladies.

Nelly exits through the door. Ada follows

Honoria picks up the minute book and reports. Vivien and Rachel stand either side of the door. Minnie, Eulalia and Honoria file past them. Minnie and Eulalia shake hands with the soon-to-depart members Honoria treats each of them to a manly pat on the shoulder

Minnie and Eulalia go out: Honoria, obviously too full to speak at parting, hurries after them

Sophie and Lilian watch the departure, then Sophie goes and kisses Lilian lightly on the cheek

Sophie Good-bye, Rachel. Good luck. (*She turns quickly and takes Vivien in her arms*)

Rachel Thank you for many kindnesses.

Sophie (*to Vivien*) Serve the Cause. Be happy. (*She kisses her*) And think of us sometimes.

Vivien Often and often. And I'll write to you. Every day . . .

Sophie (*placing a finger on her lips*) Make no rash promises. I'm glad you found Richard. (*The thought seems to disturb her. She looks towards Lilian*) I'll see you presently. (*With them watching her, she moves forlornly towards the stairs. Then she stops, turns an unfocused gaze around the room and repeats vaguely*) Presently . . .

Sophie exits up the stairs

Lilian She gets stranger every day. I'm really worried about her. But I must go and so must you. Good-bye, Rachel. (*She holds out her hand*)

Rachel (*taking Lilian's proffered hand*) Good-bye, Mrs Malin.

Lilian (*turning to Vivien*) And I'll be in London two days from now. I'll call at Lady Davey's as soon as I arrive. Don't you dare get married until I come.

Vivien No, Mother. I wouldn't think of it.

Lilian (*taking Vivien's face between her hands*) I often dreamed about your wedding but never imagined anything like this. (*She kisses her, releases her*) But he is a fine young man. It will be all right. (*She smiles at them both*) I'll see you in London.

Lilian exits through the door

Vivien gazes after Lilian, then seeks to dispel the prevailing mood of parting and regret by assuming an air of briskness

Vivien Would you wait here, Rachel? My luggage is at the station. I've just to get a small bag from my room.

Rachel (*automatically, and making no attempt to shed the prevailing mood*) Yes, of course.

Vivien I won't be long.

Vivien hurries upstairs

Rachel miserably moves the chairs back to their accustomed positions. In growing distress, she goes over to the settee

Rachel Oh, Reuben! Reuben! (*She covers her face with her hands, flops on to the settee and weeps*)

Down the stairs comes Sophie wearing her outdoor clothes and an air of purpose. She goes busily through the door to return a moment later carrying a can of the type used to contain paraffin. Briskly, she goes to the front door and goes out slamming it behind her. At the sound, Rachel jerks upright and looks in the direction of the front door.

In the street. Sophie halts, glances back at the house and then looks ahead

Sophie Oh, yes, I still have things to do—most important things.

Sophie hurries off through the arch

Rachel dries her eyes on her handkerchief, puts it away and sits staring bleakly into an unhappy future

In the street. There is the sound of drunken singing. Josiah comes through the arch looking outraged. He halts and looks behind him to the source of the maudlin singing

Josiah For God's sake, stop that bloody noise!

Reuben, happily and vocally drunk, comes into view

Reuben I can sing and dance because I've won me bet. (*And he proceeds to lurch and totter in a travesty of dancing*)

Josiah This country can never hold up its head again! This city of Manchester is for ever disgraced before the world! It has rejected one of the truly great men of our time! I'm ashamed of being a Liberal. That's what I am—ashamed!

Reuben's lurchings bring him close to Josiah and he clutches him for support

Reuben I tole yer, diden I? Tole yer that the sufferer—sufferer—those women would beat him. But you wooden lissen. You wooden *lissen!* And now you owe me fifty sovrin.

Josiah I know. I know. I'm not disputing it.

Reuben When you going to pay me? (*Breathing directly into Josiah's face*) When you going to . . .

Josiah (*backing away from him with a gesture of disgust*) I don't carry that much money around with me.

Reuben (*insistent*) *When you going to pay me?*

Josiah (*exasperated*) Oh, wait here. I won't be a minute. (*Taking out his key and muttering as he goes, he dashes to the front door, opens it and hastens within. Reuben continues his clumsy dance, stumbles, falls and sits looking contemplative*)

Rachel swivels towards the front door at the sound of the key in the lock and sits petrified as she watches Josiah angrily approaching the door

No decent man would expect to be paid—but I'll pay him—oh, yes, I'll pay him . . . (*He passes through the door*)

Hand to mouth, Rachel looks in front of her expressing doubt and fear. She rises and is creeping towards the stairs when a noise beyond the door sends her scurrying back to the settee. She throws herself down behind it face downwards, huddling to make herself as small as possible and covering her ears with her hands

Josiah comes trotting through the door carrying a small canvas bag

Blood money! Blood money, that's what it is! It won't do him a bit of good—please God!

Josiah goes out to the street slamming the front door and Rachel scrambles to a kneeling position. She leans back against the settee registering relief

In the street. Reuben hauls himself unsteadily to his feet when he sees

Josiah approaching. Josiah halts some distance from Reuben and, holding the bag at arm's length, thrusts it in the direction of the swaying man

Here's your money, Judas.

Reuben (*taking the bag and fondling it*) You won't insult me by calling me names—as long as you give me the money.

Josiah Don't you want to count it?

Reuben No, I trust you.

Josiah That money was hard come by and this time tomorrow, you'll have spent the lot—most of it on drink.

Reuben That's where you're wrong! Not this time! I'm going straight home and I'm giving this to Rachel *intact!* I'm taking her to Scarborough with it.

Josiah What! Scarborough at this time of year! She'll freeze to bloody death!

Reuben Not if she wraps up warm, she won't.

Lilian comes through the arch and Reuben, who sees her first, greets her with raised hat and a deep, if wavering bow. Josiah's greeting is more restrained. He enters into an inaudible explanation then points to Reuben who ecstatically hugs the bag to his bosom. The three of them engage in general conversation which is occasionally animated but remains unheard

In the house. Vivien appears and descends the stairs carrying a medium-sized travelling bag in one hand and an addressed envelope in the other. She is puzzled when she does not at once see Rachel

Vivien Rachel . . . (*Now she does see her*) What are you doing there?

Rachel Hiding from your father. (*She rises and brushes down her skirt with her hands*) He was here a moment ago.

Vivien Where is he now?

Rachel He went out—through the front door.

Vivien That's all right then. He probably came back for something. We were lucky he didn't burst in during the meeting.

Rachel I must say you take it very calmly.

Vivien How else should I take it? He's been—he's gone. Everything seems strange to me tonight—leaving this—going to London—going to be married . . . (*She goes over to the fireplace*) I'd better leave this where he can see it. (*She places the envelope in a prominent position on the mantelpiece*)

Rachel I left Reuben a note—I only hope he's sober enough to read it.

Vivien's comprehensive glance ranges the room and is eloquent of farewell

Vivien My father will never allow me to come home again—not when he knows I'm a suffragette—a militant.

Rachel What about your mother?

Vivien That's something else. (*She sighs*) Oh, well—let us go. (*Carrying her bag, she moves towards the front door*)

Rachel collects her bag and follows

(*As she enters the street*) I can't imagine what it will be like to be —(*she sees the talking group and ends tamely and lamely*)—married.

In the street. Vivien and Rachel stand aghast and the trio, undisturbed, continue to talk as before. Then Lilian sees the intruders and desperately waves them back to the house. Josiah shows signs of looking round, but Lilian pulls him back into the conversation. With exaggerated caution, the two women reach the front door and enter the house

In the house. Vivien closes the door and they back carefully into the room where they pause

Phoo! That was a near thing! We almost walked into him.

Rachel And that was Reuben talking to them.

Vivien That's right.

Rachel (*moving to the room door*) Come on then.

Vivien and Rachel exit through the door

In the street. Lilian breaks up the small group, moving a little apart

Lilian All I can say is that it sounds a stupid bet to me.

Reuben (*gloating as he holds up his bag*) You can hardly expect me to agree with you.

Lilian No, I congratulate you, Reuben, on taking full advantage of what must have been—(*she sweeps Josiah with a scornful glance*)— a very tempting situation. Good night. (*And she sweeps off to let herself into the house with her key, leaving the front door open*)

Josiah You've landed me in a load of trouble, Reuben, and no mistake. She'll not forget this in a hurry.

Reuben Oh, she'll be all right. (*He backs unsteadily in the direction of the arch*) I'll send you a postcard—two postcards—from Scarborough.

Reuben reels with a kind of urgency through the arch

Josiah looks apprehensively towards the house, starts for the front door, then suddenly halts in his tracks

Josiah What was I doing paying him? He *owes* me more than fifty pounds! (*He braces himself as if to face an onslaught and enters the house by the front door*)

Lilian, erect, angry, menacing, is awaiting Josiah, standing with her back to the fireplace

Lilian I wouldn't have thought you were in a position to throw away fifty pounds but I suppose you'll say it's none of my business.

Josiah Now come, Lilian, I know it looks silly now but, at the time . . .

Lilian You can't possibly justify 'such extravagant and foolish behaviour.

Josiah If you'd only listen! I just wanted to demonstrate my faith in Winston Churchill. I'm not sorry I did it. I'm sorry—and ashamed—that North Manchester has shown itself to be a nest of traitors and turncoats.

Lilian If you had asked me, I could have told you that, once the suffragettes had entered the struggle, he was bound to lose. But you'd never think of consulting me.

Josiah Not in a matter of this sort. You've got to remember that, after Sir Walter, I'm the leading Liberal in this town.

Lilian Oh, you're Liberal all right—so Liberal that you throw away your money with both hands.

Josiah That's enough, Lilian! That's enough! Right or wrong, a man's got to be master in his own house. It's a high time you remember your Bible studies. What does the Good Book say? "Thy desire shall be to thy husband and he shall rule over thee." Genesis, Chapter Three, Verse Sixteen.

Lilian The Good Book—what else does it say? "Seest thou a man wise in his own conceit? There is more hope of a fool than him." Proverbs, Chapter Twenty-six, Verse Twelve.

Lilian inclines her head in his direction as if in dismissal, climbs the stairs, and exits with great dignity

Josiah stands momentarily speechless with rage, then rushes up the stairs

Josiah Are you calling me a fool?

Josiah bounds after Lilian and exits round the bend of the stairs

In the street. Sophie, bedraggled, dishevelled, hat awry and with her face blackened, comes running through the arch. She is almost at the end of her tether but is struggling towards the front door when P.C. Thomas Dougan comes pounding after her. He seizes her by the shoulder, spins her round, registers satisfaction and marches her off through the arch.

A brief silence is broken by the sound of a train whistle which, plain and regretful, calls through the night

Through the arch comes Reuben. In one hand, hanging seemingly nerveless, at his side, he carries an open letter. He looks crushed and broken. His unfocused eyes are staring ahead as he sings tonelessly

Reuben She's a bright lass and a bonny lass
And she loves her beer
And they call her Cushey Butterfield
And I wish she was here.

Singing, Reuben passes across the front of the house and goes off R

In the house. Josiah, having shed his overcoat and hat and loosened his tie, comes down the stairs. He goes to the sideboard, pours himself a drink and samples it as he makes his way over to the fireplace. He sees the envelope, puts down his drink on the mantelpiece and picks up the envelope. Desperately, he tears it open and raises a stricken face when he has read the letter. He is still for a shocked moment or two. Then he rushes up the stairs shouting as he goes

Josiah Lilian!

Josiah exits up the stairs

(*off*) Lilian!

The lights fade

CURTAIN

ACT III

Late afternoon, the following day

When the CURTAIN *rises, both street and house are lit. In the house, Lilian is sitting on the settee. The small table is close beside her, and on it are a cup and saucer*

In the street. Nelly enters through the arch. She is wearing outdoor clothes and carrying a small suitcase. Despondently she takes out her key, opens the front door, and goes into the house

Lilian looks up as Nelly enters the room

Lilian Did they let you see her, Nelly?

Nelly No, Mrs Malin. I had no better luck than you did. (*She sets down the suitcase*)

Lilian You told them that you had brought some toilet articles and a few necessaries?

Nelly Yes. That Inspector Arkwright said Miss Sophie wasn't to have them. Because of the seriousness of the charge, he said.

Lilian I should have known better than to have let you go. After last night, they're hardly likely to be in a forgiving mood.

Nelly Both ways I passed the new Town Hall, mum. At least, I passed where it used to be. There's hardly any of it left standing and what there is—well—it's just a blackened shell.

Lilian Yes, it is a thousand pities that she was caught at the moment when she had achieved her greatest success. (*She wipes her eyes with her handkerchief*)

Nelly You shouldn't have gone, mum. You shouldn't have gone to the court this morning.

Lilian Miss Sophie is my only surviving cousin and my dearest friend. I had to go in case there was anything . . . (*Again she wipes her eyes*) There was no need for you to go, Nelly.

Nelly Oh, yes, there was. Miss Sophie is my dearest friend, too.

Lilian She'll get a long sentence. No doubt of that. She'll be an old woman when she comes out.

Nelly Yes, I thought of that. The—the master isn't back, is he, mum?

Lilian No. He hasn't returned.

Nelly With respect, mum, *he* didn't have to go there this morning.

Lilian No, Nelly, he didn't. He could have sent his regrets and everybody would have understood. But he conceived it to be his duty.

Nelly His duty! His own wife's cousin!

Lilian. In a sense, he's right—when Alderman Martin is absent, he is the Chief Magistrate.

Nelly I suppose so. But he had no call to say what he did. (*She stands up very straight with her arms at her sides and recite: with an echo of Josiah's delivery*) "Arson is one of the most serious crimes in the criminal calendar. The present example is a most exaggerated and pointless crime carried out in the mistaken belief that it will advance the cause of women's suffrage. These misguided women will learn to their cost that the Government is not to be intimidated by threats or acts of violence."

Lilian You need not have repeated it. I shall remember it as long as I live. But you missed out the last bit: "In view of the seriousness of the charge, bail is refused and the accused will be committed to the next Assizes." The accused!

Nelly Have you had anything, mum?

Lilian I made a cup of tea.

Nelly (*inspecting the cup*) Yes, but you haven't touched it.

Lilian I did start to make some sandwiches but I hadn't the heart . . .

Nelly Leave it to me. You've got to eat something to keep your strength up. (*She picks up the cup and saucer and pauses at the door*) I was very glad to find you are one of us.

Nelly goes out

Lilian He looked as if he enjoyed it.

The telephone rings. Lilian rises and goes over to answer it

Hello . . . Yes, this is Alderman Malin's house. This is Mrs Malin speaking . . . Yes—I am expecting him. Who is it? Can I give him a message? . . . (*It seems she can—and it is in an unpleasant one. Disgustedly, she holds the handset at arm's length before restoring it to its rest. She returns to the settee and sits again*)

After a moment, Nelly enters with a plate of sandwiches

Nelly Here you are, Mrs Malin. (*She places the sandwiches on the small table*) But I think you ought to have a proper meal. It can't do any good . . .

Lilian I'll be all right, Nelly. Just leave the sandwiches.

Nelly See that you eat them then. (*She turns to go, then hesitates*) I know where he is—the master, I mean.

Lilian I think I can guess. He's at the Liberal Club doing his best to drown his uneasiness and his guilt.

Nelly That's right, mum. Oh, I was proud of Miss Sophie.

Lilian So was I. Especially after—after Mr Malin had refused her bail. The way she lifted her head as she spoke . . . "You can send me to prison but there are thousands like me—all determined to fight on until women have the vote." My poor Sophie! She is so unfitted to face a prison sentence.

Nelly I'll make some tea, mum.

Lilian No hurry.

Nelly goes out

Lilian reaches out to take a sandwich, changes her mind, and thrusts the plate away from her

> *In the street. Josiah comes slowly through the arch, pausing to look behind him in puzzled, uneasy fashion. Clearly, he has been drinking and he looks troubled and shifty. Shrugging away his misgivings, he faces the house and visibly braces himself as for an encounter. He strides to the front door and lets himself into the house with his key.*

Lilian looks up as Josiah comes into the room. For a moment they regard each other like adversaries

Josiah So you didn't wait for me?

Lilian No, I didn't wait.

Josiah It would have looked better if you had. There's feeling against me in this town. I need all the help and support I can get at a time like this.

Lilian So, I imagine, does Sophie. But she didn't get any. We weren't allowed to see her.

Josiah They were right not to let you see her. She'll go to prison. She's a criminal. She's done wrong.

Lilian And I suppose you believe you've done right?

Josiah Most certainly I have. I've done my duty. (*He notices the sandwiches*) Are they beef or ham?

Lilian What? I've no idea—Nelly made them.

Josiah takes a sandwich and nibbles it experimentally

Josiah (*appreciatively*) H'm, ham. (*He continues to eat the sandwiches until all are consumed, occasionally punctuating his speech by a pause in mastication and now and then using the sandwich as an ineffectual pointer to emphasize some feature of his argument*) I was suffering torment sitting there on the Bench. It was hard for me to have to sit in judgement on a member of my own family so to speak.

Lilian Hard for you! Not for a moment! I was watching you—you were relishing it!

Josiah I was *not!* I most certainly was not relishing it! I tell you I was suffering and you didn't even spare me a glance—a single glance—of sympathy.

Lilian Perhaps that was because I was glancing sympathetically at Sophie. Hers seemed to be the greater need. She's the one who will go to prison.

Josiah So she ought to! She's a suffragette, isn't she? She's the one who has been burning down buildings. She burned down the Town Hall! My Town Hall! She deserves a life sentence! I gave her a home in my own house . . .

Lilian *We* gave her a home. As I remember it, you were most reluctant that she should come to us.

Josiah Which only shows how right I was. I've always said there was something odd about her.

Lilian Yes, you have.

Josiah You're to blame, you know.

Lilian I am?

Josiah Yes. Two suffragettes—two—under this roof and you didn't even suspect. Your daughter and your cousin.

Lilian You didn't suspect either.

Josiah Oh, no! I'm too trusting altogether—that's my trouble.

Lilian You do admit to some faults then?

Josiah Certainly—I'm inclined to believe everybody is as honest and straightforward as I am. But they're not. You can see what has happened here. That woman's led our Vivien astray. And as for that Mister Richard Ward! We're lucky—we've had an escape. We might have had him as Member and only found him out afterwards. He's supporting the suffragettes—harbouring them—encouraging them. Our Vivien has only herself to blame. She'll find out too late what sort he is.

Lilian That's one of the dangers of marriage.

Josiah What is?

Lilian Finding out what the other is like—afterwards.

Josiah You're not much of a comfort to me, are you, Lilian? You've no idea what it's been like since the case ended this morning. The rest of the Bench were barely civil when I came away. I was booed as I came out of the police court. Nobody spoke to me. Nobody greeted me in the street. I went to the Liberal Club but nobody would have a drink with me. Amos Braithwaite—never known to refuse a free drink—turned his back on me. On me! Then I come here—to this. And all because I did my public duty.

Lilian (*rising*) Surely you realize by now it is because you have done your public duty that people turn their backs on you. Sophie had broken the law. She was bound to be punished whoever sat on the Bench. So there was no need for you to go to court this morning. The tactful thing would have been to stay away but you never had any tact—that's why you've never been more than a second-rate person.

Josiah Second-rate! You'll take that back, Lilian. I'm not second-rate.

Lilian Very well. I take it back.

Josiah I should think so.

Lilian If I'm going to be strictly truthful, I ought to say third-rate.

Josiah (*dangerously calm*) I see. I see what you're trying to do—you're trying to provoke me so that you can avoid discussion of your responsibility—your responsibility as a mother. If I were a second- or third-rate person, I would not have achieved the position I hold in this town.

Lilian I wouldn't bet on that.

Josiah All right. All right. I'll remind you of this a little later on. You'll come to your senses and, when you do, you're in for a shock. Do you know what this lot could mean? I'll be lucky if I *am* Mayor in October. I could be asked to resign.

Lilian It's not the end of the world if they do ask you to resign.

Josiah Not the end of the . . . ! I know this much: you'll be a very disappointed woman if you aren't Mayoress.

Lilian That's where you're wrong, Josiah. (*She snaps her fingers*) I don't give that for being Mayoress.

Josiah's jaw drops in astonishment. He gazes at her speechlessly and is forced to swallow before he can speak

Josiah I'm beginning to think that I don't understand you, Lilian.

Lilian That's the only perceptive observation I've known you make in ten years. (*She considers*) In fifteen years.

Nelly comes in with a cup of tea on a tray. She is going over to Lilian but has to pass close to Josiah. He checks her and takes the cup. Nelly looks surprised but shrugs and goes out again

Josiah Then I've been wrong all this time. You don't care whether I'm Mayor or not.

Lilian Let us put it this way—I think there are more important things in life.

Josiah I see. I see. (*He sits and sips his tea without enjoyment*) Quite a few things fit into place now.

Lilian That's something gained then. (*She moves in the direction of the stairs*) I'm going out.

Josiah Where are you going?

Lilian I'll tell you when I come down.

Josiah It has nothing to do with Vivien, has it? Because I warn you, Lilian, I won't have any more to do with her. I won't have her name mentioned in this house.

Lilian She's still my daughter. I'm not prepared to give any undertaking.

Josiah After what she's done, after what she wrote to me in her letter, she's lost to me.

Lilian I see. (*She starts to ascend the stairs*)

Josiah Lilian . . .

Lilian (*turning*) Yes?

Josiah Do you know why I went to court this morning? The real reason?

Lilian Since you so obviously intend to tell me . . . (*She waits with ill-concealed impatience*)

Josiah I wanted to show them what I thought of the suffragettes— to show them that I wouldn't budge from my principles even if my own family was involved.

Lilian You have shown them and you know what they think of you.

Lilian exits upstairs

Josiah Listen, Lilian . . .

Josiah is about to follow her when the telephone rings. The tea-cup is still in his hand and he puts it down before picking up the handset

Hello. Hello . . . Will you speak up, please? Yes, this is Alderman Malin speaking . . . (*We see his face as he listens at some length and it expresses growing anger and consternation*) How dare you? How dare you speak to me like that? You're a public nuisance, that's what you are and I shall report this—this intrusion to the police.

Josiah hangs up. But he is considerably disquieted for he mutters angrily, comes over to the settee and sits down. He reflects briefly and, muttering again, glances back to the telephone. A noise above stairs brings him to his feet

Lilian enters downstairs. She is wearing her outdoor clothes and seems suddenly more dignified and formidable than the woman who lately left the room. Her bearing is erect, her expression is calm and dedicated, and she wears with tremendous effect, the purple, green and white sash of the Women's Social and Political Union. Two stairs from the bottom, with her hand on the rail, she halts and gazes down on Josiah's astonished, upturned face

(*pointing*) What's that thing?

Lilian This sash proclaims me as a member of the Women's Social and Political Union.

Josiah Here, what's this? What's this?

Lilian Not what's this but who's this? I am Hippolyta.

Josiah Oh, no! *No!*

His shouted negative is both a denial and a plea. Lilian gravely nods in dignified confirmation

Lilian I'd like you to know that I have brought no influence to bear on either Vivien or Sophie. They didn't know I was Hippolyta until last night. Both of them became suffragettes entirely of their own accord.

Josiah I don't know what I've done—I don't know why this should happen to me. I've always been a good husband and father . . . .

Lilian shakes her head

Do you mean I haven't?

Lilian Definitely not! As a husband, you've been a tyrant. As a father, you've been a bully.

Josiah But I've always been known as a kind man . . .

Lilian By those who didn't have to live with you. We've known you as domineering, self-opinionated, over-bearing and narrow-minded.

Josiah No, Lilian, no! You're going too far! You're letting yourself be carried away. Everybody acknowledges that I'm a generous man.

Lilian Yes, you are generous.

Josiah There! You've got to admit . . .

Lilian In the material sense, you are generous. In every other sense, you are mean—mean-spirited. You lack understanding, sensitivity and sympathy. And now I'm going.

Josiah (*moving towards the stairs*) You're not leaving this house.

Lilian Oh, yes, I am—and you won't stop me.

She descends one more stair and he gives back a little

Josiah If you leave this house, you don't come back.

Lilian That is just what I intend—not to come back.

Josiah You're leaving me?

Lilian Yes. You'll agree, I think, that it is the best thing. There is to be a suffragette demonstration in sympathy with Sophie's arrest. You are to be one of the targets of the demonstration.

Josiah I am? You can stand there and tell me so! And you'll do nothing to stop them?

Lilian Nothing. (*She moves past him and turns*) Not a thing. Whatever happens to you, you have deserved it over and over again.

Josiah This sort of behaviour won't get you the vote.

Lilian Tell us what will—because we're determined to have it. We've tried the appeal to reason. It is time now for other measures. Good-bye, Josiah.

Josiah Good-bye—like that? Twenty-seven years. Twenty-seven years of marriage, Lilian. Don't they mean anything to you?

Lilian Yes, they do. (*She reflects*) Oppression—misery—and, yes—boredom.

Josiah is deeply shocked. He stands staring helplessly at Lilian

Lilian turns from him and goes purposefully through the room and hall. She opens the front door, slams it behind her and, at the same brisk pace, passes under the arch

Only when the reverberating door-slam echoes through the house does Josiah stir. He makes a small detaining gesture and then, realizing how ineffective it is, goes over to the sideboard and pours himself a whisky. He drifts to the settee, sits and sips his drink

Josiah I've always tried to be a good husband and a good father. Always . . . (*But he sounds troubled and doubtful. He applies himself to his drink again*)

Nelly enters through the door. Like Lilian, she is wearing her outdoor clothes and the sash of the Women's Social and Political Union

Nelly (*moving sideways behind Josiah towards the front door*) I've left you cold meat, pickles, bread 'n cheese and an apple pie, Mr Malin.

Josiah (*apathetic*) All right, Nelly. (*Then, suddenly realizing*) Here, where are you going? (*He turns, sees her and rises*) What the hell is going on?

Nelly I am a member of the Executive Committee of the Metringham branch of the Women's Social and Political Union. By arrangement with Mrs Malin I ceased to be in your employment from four o'clock this afternoon, sir.

Josiah Then what the hell are you doing in my house? Get out! Get out at once!

Nelly I'll be glad to. I've hated it here. (*She moves towards the hall and turns back to him*) If I was you, Mr Malin, I'd get out too—while you've still got a chance.

Josiah Out! *Out!* Out of here! (*He points to the front door*) This very minute!

Nelly flies from the house, slams the front door, and bolts through the arch

Disturbed and angry, Josiah prowls round the room

(*muttering to himself*) A girl of that class warning me. Warning *me!* Who does she think she is? Who're they to threaten me? I don't have to put up with this. I don't have to . . . (*A sudden thought strikes him. He hurries over to the telephone and picks it up*) Hello, operator. Give me Metringham seven-four . . . Is that the police station? It's Alderman Malin. Get me the Chief Constable on the line . . . Oh, is he? Then get me Superintendent Williamson . . . Hello, Super. Josiah Malin here. There's trouble brewing. A big demonstration of suffragettes is planned for tonight. It seems I'm to be their target . . . How do I know? My wife's just told me. It appears that, all unbeknownst to me, she's been the leader of the Metringham suffragettes . . . No, I'm not joking . . . Yes, it is surprising. Think yourself lucky you're a bachelor . . . No, I don't want sympathy—I want police protection . . . That's right. I don't think it consonant with my dignity to start fighting a mob of women. You'll see to it? . . . One little thing before you hang up —just remember who's Chairman of the Watch Committee . . . That's right. Good night. (*Smiling, he hangs up*) Now we'll see. We'll see what they do now. (*He returns to the settee with his drink*)

In the street. Headlong through the arch hurtles Inspector Nathan Arkwright. He is floundering in his stride like a man who has run beyond his limit. He flings himself upon the front door and beats

*a tattoo on the knocker. Then he looks desperately behind and repeats
the tattoo with increased violence. He fairly dances with impatience*

*At the first thunderous knocking, Josiah sets down his glass and moves
a few stealthy steps towards the front door. At the second insistent
summons, he tiptoes to the front door, opens it cautiously and peers
outside. When he sees Nathan, he flings the door open, seizes him by
the wrist and drags him into the house. Then he closes the door and goes
into the room with a surprised Nathan following*

That was quick! My word, that was quick!

Nathan I had to be quick. There was nothing else for it.

Josiah But it's only a matter of seconds since I telephoned the
Superintendent. I really must congratulate him.

Nathan The Superintendent knows nothing about it. I'm here
because I was chased down the length of Buttermarket Street by
a horde of suffragettes all wearing coloured sashes.

Josiah I rang for police protection. I've been officially warned that
I'm to be the target for a suffragette demonstration.

Nathan "Officially warned . . ." By the Superintendent?

Josiah No, by my wife. It turns out that she is Hippolyta, the leader
of the local suffragettes.

Nathan *Never!*

Josiah I do assure you. And shouldn't you be telling me? After all,
you're *supposed* to be investigating all these suffragette outrages.

Nathan I never would have believed it—never!

Josiah I've more news for you—all the women in my house: my
wife, Sophie Ormesby, our Vivien, and Nelly, our maid, are all
suffragettes. It's been going on under my nose . . .

Nathan What? All of them?

Josiah Every last one. Vivien has run off to London to marry that
young feller who came up to be Liberal candidate.

Nathan I didn't go much on him—he was too la-di-da.

Josiah He's a Southerner. My wife has left me. My daughter's run
away. I'm completely on my own. You're talking, Nathan, to a
man whose life is in ruins.

Nathan I'm very sorry. Very sorry indeed.

Josiah What's more, in this very room, not ten minutes ago, Nelly,
the girl who this morning brought my tea to the bedroom, the
girl I've seen black-leading the kitchen grate warned me—warned
me!—to get out of town while I'd got time. (*He surveys Nathan*)
There! What have you got to say to that?

Nathan I'd go. I'd go at once.

Josiah What? Run away from a pack of women?

Nathan You haven't seen them. I have. They're out for blood.

Josiah But the police—the police'll stop them.

Nathan I tell you there aren't enough of us. It's a job for the military
and they won't get here in time.

Josiah What would you do in my place?

Nathan I'd go without stopping to pack a thing. I'd go to the railway station, take a ticket to Sale and spend the night at my brother's place. Your brother's, that is.

Josiah I haven't spoken to our Sam for all of five years.

Nathan You asked me what I'd do.

Josiah Go now?

Nathan This minute—there's not a moment to be lost.

Josiah Right.

With an air of decision, Josiah strides to the front door pausing only to take his hat from the hat-stand and put it on his head. Nathan follows Josiah closely. Josiah opens the front door

In the street. Honoria comes through the arch flanked by Nelly and Minnie. They are wearing the W.S.P.U. sashes, as will all the suffragettes we are to see later. All three regard the front door with a menacing gaze. They remain in this watchful attitude while the following brief scene is played

Josiah slams the door, leans briefly against it and returns to the room, with Nathan following

That was near! My God, that was near!

Nathan You've left it too late. You should have gone when that girl told you.

Josiah Thank you very much. Have you any more suggestions?

Nathan I think we ought to have a drink.

Josiah That's the first sensible thing you've said. (*He goes to the sideboard and prepares two stiff drinks*) And I suppose I can take this hat off. (*He does so and places it on the sideboard*) I'm not going anywhere. Not yet anyway. Here.

Nathan Thanks.

Nathan accepts the glass and, as if moved by a common impulse, they walk over to the settee where they sit—occasionally sipping their drinks and staring despondently ahead

In the street. Honoria is the first to relax her watchful attitude. The other two quickly follow suit

Honoria Pity about that. However, we'll have them out in no time. No time at all.

Nelly I never suspected that Mrs Malin was Hippolyta—never for a minute.

Honoria That could be because you're not very bright, Nelly.

Nelly Lady Honoria!

Honoria Or it could be because Mrs Malin is very clever. (*She smiles at Nelly*) Nobody suspected her, you silly girl.

Nelly Yes, but with me living in the same house . . .

Honoria So were Alderman Malin, Vivien and Sophie and they hadn't an inkling. So you needn't reproach yourself. (*She looks over her shoulder to the arch*) Here she comes.

Lilian comes through the arch accompanied by Eulalia and several suffragettes we have not seen before. They leave a little clear space around her

Lilian I think we all know what we have to do tonight. This demonstration is part of a nation-wide effort, but you will realize that we shall have to make a loud and continuous noise if we are to awaken a nation's conscience which has slumbered, as far as we are concerned, for a thousand years. For purely personal reasons, I cannot take part in the next phase of this particular operation so I am temporarily handing over command to Lady Honoria.

Honoria Understood. Understood, Lilian, and fully appreciated.

Lilian Now I am going to join Miss Hackney's column and we all meet in an hour for the march.

Honoria That's right—at John Bright's statue at the bottom of Bridge Street.

Lilian turns to leave but wavers and looks back at Honoria

Lilian One thing I ask. We are resolved on what we have to do but, please, no undue violence to Mr Malin.

Honoria You can trust us, Lilian.

There is a murmur of assent

> *Lilian goes off through the arch*

The suffragettes chatter while Honoria surveys them. She draws herself impressively erect

> (*in stentorian tones*) R-r-right! (*It is a fearful sound, something between summons and a command*)

Immediately the suffragettes are silenced, and automatically arrange themselves precisely in two ranks

> Any questions?

Nelly Yes. I don't really know what we're supposed to do with Mr Malin.

Honoria That's because you don't pay attention. You don't *listen!* We're going to take him and that Inspector Arkwright and duck them in the horse-trough—the very same one that Alderman Malin was public-spirited enough to present to the town.

Eulalia And with any luck, they'll be just in time to be seen and appreciated by the first-house audience leaving the Hippodrome.

Honoria (*pointing*) You two—to your posts.

Two suffragettes detach themselves, obey her pointing finger and hurry off by the R

Now let us see where a frontal attack will get us.

With the others following, Honoria walks up to the front door and beats out an imperative summons on the knocker. Then she folds her arms and waits

Josiah and Nathan rise at the knocking and move stealthily forward until they are standing close together and seem to be peering out of a window

Nathan They're out there—waiting.
Josiah I can see that for myself.
Nathan You could telephone the police station again.
Josiah I could and I will. (*He dashes over to the telephone and picks it up*) Hello, operator . . . What's that? . . . It's what? . . . Oh, I see. Then who're you? . . . I see . . . Yes, of course. (*He hangs up*)
Nathan What's the matter?
Josiah The exchange is on fire. That was a fireman. Now what?
Nathan We could always pray.
Josiah Not me! Churchill defeated! My Town Hall burned to the ground! My wife and daughter gone! Four suffragettes under my roof! (*His upward glance is heavily charged with reproach*) No! I feel I've been *let down!*

In the street. There is a diversion as P.C. Thomas Dougan backs into view from the R. He is clearly intimidated and is looking fearfully before him. The two suffragettes appear and effectively cut off his retreat in that direction. He turns to flee through the arch and visibly recoils when he sees Honoria and the rest. They withdraw from the area of the front door and move towards the arch so that he is surrounded with his back to the door. He takes an uneasy backward step. The suffragettes stand looking at him

Honoria This is the man who arrested Sophie Ormesby.

There is a wordless growl from the women as the policeman cowers. He darts a pleading glance in the direction of the house

Nathan P.C. Dougan's out there.
Josiah I'm not blind. I can see him.
Nathan Get him in here. He'd hold them off. He's a lion, that man, a lion!

Josiah rushes to the front door, opens it and calls

Josiah Dougan! This way, man!

P.C. Dougan wheels round and runs desperately towards the open door. When Josiah realizes that there is danger of admitting the women, he slams the door—right in the constable's face. Defeated, crushed, he turns to face his pursuers who regard him balefully

Honoria What have you to say for yourself?

With a sudden surge of courage, P.C. Dougan draws himself up to clear his throat and the suffragettes collectively brace themselves in expectation of a tremendous outburst. But, instead of speech, a wheezy, scared cough is heard, surprising alike to the constable and the women

Right. Deal with him but remember he is merely an instrument.

The suffragettes converge on him, engulfing him and he disappears from view. There is a mêlée with all the women pressing to the centre of it. The heaving, thrusting, pushing, tearing and dragging continues for a few moments and then Honoria's stentorian shout is heard

That's enough! Leave him *alone!*

They all give back to form once more a semicircle around the fallen man. P.C. Thomas Dougan lies on the ground without boots and without his trousers. Two of the new suffragettes each hold a boot and it is Eulalia who flourishes his trousers like a captured flag. P.C. Dougan hauls himself to his feet. He is ludicrous in dark socks and long white underpants and he tries to pull down his inadequate shirt to hide his underwear. Dumbly, he entreats the return of his trousers from Eulalia. She makes a gesture of refusal and tosses them to a suffragette who passes them on until they reach a woman on the flank

The woman exits with the trousers

All the women taking part in this teasing exercise show their empty hands. Honoria points to the arch and Dougan is about to go, when the two women holding his boots relent and present them to him

Dougan exits with a boot clutched in each hand

The lights in the street fade

In the house. Josiah and Nathan have watched the proceedings with growing terror

Josiah If he's a lion, what chance have we?
Nathan He'll never be able to lift up his head in this town! Never again! Not after this!
Josiah Come on. Let us try to get out the back way while they're round the front.

Josiah and Nathan dash out through the door and at once noises of conflict are heard. In a moment they are back inside the room—more quickly than they left it. Nathan is holding his hand to his head but desists long enough to help Josiah to drag the sideboard in front of the door. Josiah then relaxes a little but Nathan continues to nurse his injured head

The place is full of them. Full of them! Mind you, I recognized that big fat bitch who hit you over the head with her umbrella.

The lights in the room begin to fade

Nathan You ought to—it's my Annie—my wife.
Josiah Oh, I'm so sorry, Nathan.
Nathan (*rubbing his head*) Don't be. Big fat bitch will do very well.

The room grows gradually darker reflecting the increasing fears of both men. Soon all is dark around them but they are standing in a pool of light wincing and clutching each other as the noises around them grow ever more threatening

Josiah The front door will stand anything short of a battering ram.
Nathan And it will take something to move that sideboard.
Josiah Perhaps we ought to put that settee——

There is a crash beyond the door. They cling together and look in the direction of the noise

—behind the door.

They move apart

I never told them. I never told either Lilian or Vivien how much I loved them.

There is another crash. Again they look towards the door

If only we knew what they mean to do with us.
Nathan Until I saw P.C. Dougan just now I never understood what they meant by a fate worse than death.

There is the loud shattering of glass close at hand. Once more, they cling together—and separate

Josiah Here, give us a hand with that settee.

They move towards the settee but, as they do so, light strikes the staircase, revealing that it is crowded with the suffragettes—Honoria on the lowest step. The two men stand rooted to the spot

Honoria You'd better go quietly.
Josiah Just a moment. I'd like to say a word.

Honoria's sweeping gesture accords him full permission. He stands with his head thrown back—Joan of Arc at the stake, Sidney Carton at the foot of the guillotine

However much you humiliate me, I am proud to think that this
is something I share, in a measure, with Winston Churchill.

Honoria *Now!*

*In a body, the women bear down on the two men, seize them and, one of
the group having opened the front door, they are hustled out into the
lighted street and through the arch with Josiah still wearing his expression of noble resignation.*

The lights fade to a Black-Out, and music is heard for a brief moment.
*Then the lights come up again slowly to reveal that the street is
full of suffragettes with Lilian leading them. They are apparently
marching, and they are certainly carrying a banner with* VOTES
FOR WOMEN *emblazoned on it. They are singing too—a song we have
heard before*

All   Is this the land?

Is this the land where men walk free?
Is this the land of liberty?

Is this the land?

Is this the land which claims to be
The cradle of democracy?

This is the land.

This is the land where you will see
Women live in slavery.
This is the land, the land that we
Will change for our posterity.

This is the land.

Through the night, sister, through the night,
Through the night of tyranny!
To the fight, sister, to the fight!
Take my hand and come with me.

O come with me and have no fear!
The time is now! The hour is here!

O come with me!

A soaring voice takes up a new song in which all join

We shall overcome,
We shall overcome,

We shall overcome—some day.
Deep in my heart,
I do believe
We shall overcome some day.

Time is claiming the suffragettes. Light is dimming and their voices are fading. But, when the light has gone, from the darkness there comes an echo from history

We shall overcome—some day.

CURTAIN

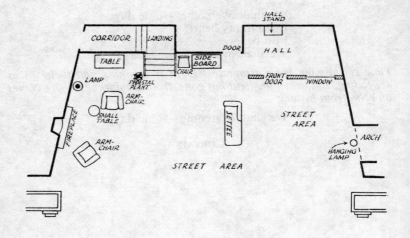

FURNITURE AND PROPERTY LIST

ACT I

On stage: Settee

2 armchairs

Table. *On it:* ornate handset telephone

Sideboard. *On it:* bottles of whisky, rum, gin, water jug, soda water, glasses, ink-bottle, pen

Pedestal plant

Small chair

Small table

Hall-stand

Carpet

Stair carpet

On mantelpiece: various ornaments

Off stage: Sheaf of papers (**Josiah**)

Inspector's stick (**Nathan**)

Bible (**Lilian**)

Tray with bowl of water, lint, bandage, scissors (**Lilian**)

Personal: **Reuben:** notebook and pencil

Josiah: key, money

Nelly: key

Sophie: key

Vivien: key

Nathan: bloodstained handkerchief

ACT II

SCENE 1

Strike: Dirty glasses
Tray with lint, etc.

Set: Small table in former position

Off stage: Suitcase (**Rachel**)
Papers and notebook (**Rachel**)
2 small parcels (**Honoria**)

Personal: **Ada:** pin-watch

SCENE 2

Off stage: Paraffin can (**Sophie**)
Small canvas bag (**Josiah**)
Travelling bag (**Vivien**)
Envelope (**Vivien**)
Open letter (**Reuben**)

Personal: **Rachel:** handkerchief

ACT III

Strike: Dirty glasses

Set: Small table by settce. *On it:* cup and saucer

Off stage: Small suitcase (**Nelly**)
Plate of sandwiches (**Nelly**)
Cup of tea (**Nelly**)

Personal: **Lilian:** handkerchief

LIGHTING PLOT

Property fittings required: standard lamp, hanging street lamp
Composite set, a room, hall and street. The same setting throughout

ACT I

To open: Street lighting up. House lighting out

Cue 1   **Richard** and **Josiah** enter house   (Page 7)
Street lighting out, house lighting up

Cue 2   Police whistles blows   (Page 10)
Street lighting up to $\frac{3}{4}$

Cue 3   **Josiah:** ". . . I have a bath"   (Page 24)
House lighting out

Cue 4   **Dougan** points at front door   (Page 24)
Black-Out

ACT II, SCENE 1

To open: House lighting up. Street lighting out

Cue 5   **Richard** enters   (Page 26)
Street lighting up to full

Cue 6   **Josiah** exits   (Page 28)
Street lighting out

Cue 7   **Honoria** and **Eulalia** enter   (Page 32)
Street lighting up

Cue 8   **Dougan** watches front door   (Page 36)
Street lighting fade, blaze briefly on Dougan's face, then out

Cue 9   **Honoria:** ". . . in listening attitudes"   (Page 40)
Street arch lamp up, then fade

Cue 10   **Ada:** ". . . timorous or faint-hearted"   (Page 44)
Street lighting up

Cue 11   **Honoria:** "This is Hippolyta"   (Page 45)
Fade to Black-Out

ACT III

To open: Black-Out

Cue 12   On CURTAIN up   (Page 45)
Bring up spot on Lilian

Cue 13   **Lilian:** ". . . bad working conditions"   (Page 45)
Bring up house lighting. Fade spot

Cue 14   **Nelly:** "It'll be our Minnie"   (Page 45)
Bring up street lighting

Cue 15   **Josiah:** "Lilian!"   (Page 53)
Fade to Black-Out

ACT III

To open: House and street lighting up

Cue 16	**Dougan** exits	**(Page 66)**
	Street lighting fades	
Cue 17	**Josiah:** ". . . with her umbrella"	**(Page 67)**
	House lighting begins to fade: continue until dark except for spot on Nathan and Josiah	
Cue 18	**Josiah:** ". . . with the settee"	**(Page 67)**
	Lighting up on stairs and in street	
Cue 19	Crowd exits with **Josiah**	**(Page 68)**
	Black-Out, then bring up street lighting	
Cue 20	**Suffragettes:** . . . "We shall overcome"	**(Page 69)**
	Fade to Black-Out	

EFFECTS PLOT

ACT I

ACT II

SCENE 1

SCENE 2

ACT III

ESSEX COUNTY LIBRARY

DRAMA SECTION .... LIBRARY

This book is to be returned on or before the last date above.

It may be borrowed for a further period if not in demand.